PULAOS AND BIRYANIS

A TRIBUTE TO INDIAN CUISINE

PULAOS AND BIRYANIS

A Tribute to Indian Cuisine

KATY DALAL

VAKILS, FEFFER AND SIMONS PVT. LTD.
Hague Building, 9, Sprott Road, Ballard Estate
Mumbai 400 001

First printing 2002
Second printing 2003

Price: Rs. 245/-

ISBN 81-87111-52-6

Published by
Bimal A. Mehta for
Vakils, Feffer and Simons Pvt. Ltd.
Hague Building, 9, Sprott Road,
Ballard Estate, Mumbai 400 001.

Printed by
Arun K. Mehta at
Vakil & Sons Pvt. Ltd., Industry Manor,
Appasaheb Marathe Marg, Worli,
Mumbai 400 025.

Photographs: Jamshed K. Billimoria
Cover page Design: K. R. Billimoria
Photograph facing Page 33 : Arish Patel

To the memory of

my dearest friend

SHIREEN GAZDAR

who saw me through a dark period in my life. She always encouraged me to move to greater heights and by her simplicity and forthrightness taught me to be firm and brave to face all the vicissitudes of life.

I bear her loss with deep sorrow.

CONTENTS

INTRODUCTION

Nowhere in the world is rice so treasured and valued as in India. In fact, the whole of South-East Asia is a rice belt with hundreds of varieties grown and rice forms the staple diet of people in Thailand, Vietnam, China, Indonesia and other countries. But the way in which the Moghul rulers in India developed its cooking and presentation was an art form. The rice was cooked in a phenomenal manner. It was studded with flower petals, essences, nuts, eggs and fabulous spices. The rice covered mutton, chicken, wild game and vegetables all cooked in sauces containing curds, cream, milk, ground almonds and pistachios and then the whole was placed in silver or golden dishes, depending on the ruler or noble's wealth and covered with thin, wispy sheets of beaten silver and gold. This gorgeous display sometimes had roasted peacocks along with their feathers serving as decorative items on pulao salvers.

We have this tradition passed on to us by the courts of Lucknow, Awadh and Hyderabad. The households of noblemen revolved around their "Dastarkhwan". The various chefs would vie with each other to produce original recipes so that their masters could proudly speak of the wonders emerging from their kitchens. From Awadh comes the story of a live bird flying out from a fried puri. It reminds me of the song learnt in Junior School of "four and twenty blackbirds baked in a pie, when the pie was opened the birds began to sing...."

There is a marked difference between Lucknowi and Hyderabadi foods. Numerous Lucknowi dishes consist of ground mutton compared to Hyderabadi food which uses a great deal of minced mutton in its rice preparations.

There seems little doubt that the Moghuls brought their food to Hyderabad, where it got assimilated with the local Deccani cuisine. Other influences on Hyderabadi food came from visiting foreigners such as the Arabs, the Egyptians, the Europeans and the Negroes who made up a part of the Nizam's security guard. It was the latter who were responsible for the delicious creation called "Patthar – Ka – Gosht". Many gourmets feel that it was the Persians who brought the kababs to Hyderabad and its accompanying biryanis. The old cadre of family cook is dying out. The present young ones are learning new trades.

The Hyderabadi food is a highly aromatic, chilli-hot food. Even its biryanis use earthy, tangy, mind-boggling hot spices such as various coloured chillies, black peppercorns, cinnamon, cardamom, tamarind, coriander, ginger, garlic and mint. They use less saunf or variali or fennel. The biryanis consist of the flesh of different types of game, the favourite being wild boar. The southern influences come from four quarters, Andhra Pradesh, Tamil Nadu, Karnataka and Kerala.

The Hyderabadi loved burning hot mango and lemon pickles in oil and always had a variety of chutneys with ginger, garlic, raw mangoes, tomatoes, chilli pickle, and tamarind chutney. There were also mixed vegetable pickles.

There is even a recipe called Mirchi – Salan offered at the end of a sumptuous meal to aid digestion. You bite into a piping hot chilli and out gushes a stream of hot-sour sauce enough to blow you out of your mind.

This Hyderabadi food involved a great deal of pain and "Mehnat" or effort. It is a very creative cuisine and without exaggeration one could easily qualify it as the most exotic cuisine of India. The thought at its basic creation was to assault all one's senses. One did not blanch on eating it — one revelled and indulged in the excess of its hot, sour, tangy, piercing tastes.

In comparison Moghlai cuisine emphasized on lightness in colour and cooking. The tastes were more delicate. There was an emphasis on the use of saffron, ground almonds and pistachios, the use of raisins and dried fruits, the use of flower petals and violent itters and Kewra or screw pine essence. The northern Kashmiri food could not be separated from cumin, cloves, fresh or dried ginger and asafoetida.

The coastal fare of the South of India and the Konkan could not be separated from the coconut. It was used in ground form, milk form, or oil form in practically every single recipe. The baghar or tadka or seasoning could not be separated from curry leaves, mustard seeds and fenugreek seeds. The Parsi food could never be divorced from its chopped onion and its ginger-garlic paste which was used in the cooking of mutton, chicken, duck and even vegetables. Punjabi food was delicious cooked in pure ghee or mustard oil. Cream, paneer and dahi were its major ingredients along with Ma-Ki-Dal and layered parathas streaming in ghee. Gajar-Ka-Halwa and Meethe-wale-Chaval dripped sugar syrup and mawa.

Geography plays a great importance on food tastes. The Goans went in for fish in a very big way. Added to that, they cooked immense amounts of pork vindaloo and sorpotel in chillies and hot spices ground in vinegar.

The Saraswat Brahmins of the Konkan coast made sweets and savouries from every conceivable vegetable and even fruits and excelled in seafood preparations such as Bombay Ducks, Mussels, Oysters, Lobsters, Prawns, Baby Octopus, Baby Sharks, Pomfrets, Rawas, Surmai and Crabs.

The Bengali too loved his fish and vegetables, although he ate mutton, beef and pork and had a taste for Chinese foods. He often ate mixed vegetables with a little bitter vegetable thrown in for taste. The Coorgi loved his pork, the Keralite his fish, the Andhraite his chillies and the man from Karnataka could not be separated from his coconuts. The Moplahs of the Malabar coast, too, use similar spices like the Hyderabadis in their fish and mutton dishes with the ubiquitous coconut.

Anglo-Indian and East Indian food preparations are to a great extent influenced by the cuisine of the English Memsahib in India. They have, cutlets and potato patties and soups and desserts, meats, chicken recipes and puddings catering to Western tastes to a large extent. But they did not give up their Indian curries, chillies and pickles.

The middle and lower classes are content as far as their appetites are well looked after but on the opposite rung we have the poorest of India's poor subsisting on thick glutinous rice, day after day, for all of their lives. I have seen paddy husked by an almost hundred year old woman in her little hut. She sat on the floor and pounded the paddy and winnowed it. She did not bother to wash the rice but placed the required amount in a terracotta vessel called "Penni", poured water in it and placed it on a wooden fire she lit with dried date leaves. She allowed the rice to boil and boil until the water turned milky with the starch. This liquid called "Page" was emptied into another clay vessel and drunk by the old woman and her older husband. I tried some. It tasted like muddy gum. The rice was eaten with pounded red chillies and a dried, baked Bombay Duck.

So much diversity exists in the methods of cooking rice in India. Suffice it to say that the whole of South-East Asia is nourished by it. In every rice growing country various items are cooked along with rice; but none of them can compare with the fabulous pulaos and biryanis cooked by our Indian chefs who work in palaces, hotels, private houses and even along the wayside dhabas.

My paternal grand-mother Cooverbai Frenchman had lived in Rawalpindi in the North-West Frontier (now in Pakistan), for many years. Her sister-in-law, a very great and grand lady, Meherbai Boga seated almost fifty people everyday at her lavish table. Food was cooked by three trained men and from eating, seeing and watching them at their duties, she quietly and seriously resolved to learn all she could.

Her first advice to me at the age of eight was that the most delicious foods were cooked over a slow heat. "Do not try to place your dekchi or tapeli on high heat for this will burn your gravy a lot faster than it should and the meat would remain dry and only be partially cooked".

The second piece of advice was to place a cover on the vessel holding the meat and pour water on it. Regularly stir the meat and replace the water which would evaporate in the vessel.

The minute you use the word pulao or biryani it conjures up a picture of good pinkish red goat's mutton. Some people use shoulder mutton for mince as well as the neck portion called pallu. For myself I prefer the mutton for the rice dishes to be from the leg portion along with the nali bones. These nali bones are thought to be the most tasty portion of the goat as they contain white or black narrow which is highly prized by epicureans. In fact if your butcher agrees to provide, and you can afford to pay for it, collect one or two kilograms of nali and make it into the beautiful pulao recipe I have given in this book.

The pulao and biryani mutton takes hours to cook because Indian goat meat is tough and stringy. So depending on where you live, you marinade it with dahi or curds or green, raw papaya along with its skin mashed into pulp. The papaya contains properties to tenderize the meat, so that it cooks faster.

There is a superior type of mutton available in India if you should be so lucky as to get it. I'm afraid only a few fortunate people get to eat what is known as "Kurbani-Ka-Mutton". The best quality of large goats are especially fattened for the muslim families for their ID festivals. The goats come down in thousands from Rajasthan. Sometimes amongst these there will be one or two animals whose backs will mysteriously bear the words "Allah", "Mohammed", "Ya Allah", "La Illaha" and these are pure white with the names in chocolate coloured hair. These unusual animals are often 50 kg. or over in weight and are bought by film stars, rich bhaiyas, rich memons — Patels, Mansuris — who are very rich and spiritually inclined people. The monetary range of such goats goes upto one lakh of rupees and even upto one and a half lakh of rupees. The goat is cut up in private and it is distributed in the name of Allah. Actually the "Bakra" as the goat is called is roughly divided into three parts. The first portion in the name of Allah is divided between poor families or sent to orphanages or "Yatim Khanas", the second portion is distributed between relatives and the third portion is kept for the household.

Traditional terms exist to describe the various steps taken by the great chefs in their cooking of pulaos and biryanis. The first step would be to fry the onions and then the masalas very slowly so that they don't stick to the bottom of the pan. One step is deep frying whole masalas to allow their essence to flow into the ghee.

Another pulao is the dum method, where the pulao is put in a vessel in layers, then covered with a tight lid and fresh dough to seal in the aromas. Then it is placed on an iron tava over a medium flame for fifteen to thirty minutes depending on how much the rice has been cooked.

There is yet another method, which I rarely follow, but which it is believed old-fashioned chefs used a great deal. They placed live coals either directly upon the biryani rice or on separated onionskins or in a stainless steel katori. Then ghee is poured over the live coals so a great deal of smoke is created. The lid is quickly placed on the vessel and it is then sealed with dough so that the smoke is trapped in the vessel. Some people also put a pinch of asafoetida on the coals whilst others pour a little bit of the biryani gravy itself on top. Some place dry spices along with the ghee.

In today's world, practically nobody uses coal in their small flats. Especially not in the fancy large kitchens of Cuffe Parade, Malabar Hill and Bandra. Unless you have a garden where you can happily use a tandoor and as many sigris as needed, this type of cookery using coal is a total no-no. Ofcourse some traditionalist kitchens may be using this method, but by and large it is a disappearing trait.

THE MODERN WOMAN'S METHOD OF DEALING WITH THE DEMANDS OF COOKING PULAOS AND BIRYANIS

The electric rice cooker is one of the most marvelous gadgets invented for harried and tired housewives. It is simple and clean to use, does not stain your vessels and gives you beautiful danedar rice within 30 to 35 minutes. If you do not possess one, do go out and buy one. All the lovely recipes in this book will magically be created by you in minutes or an hour or so at the most. You need not be threatened by having to face your husband's friends for a meal or be frightened when you have unexpected guests. Armed with your rice and pressure cookers you will be able to conquer mountains. All your culinary worries will vanish and you will be able to bring joy to your family with this plethora of fabulous dishes, which once upon a time would have taken half a day to prepare.

So I wish you lots of luck in preparing the rice dishes in this book many of which have been adapted from old royal recipes.

Never worry about how things will turn out. Each woman has her own way of doing things. Some people dislike sugar in their food — so omit it. Some people dislike turmeric — omit it. Some people don't like whole spices in their food — so don't omit them — tie them in a muslin bag and allow to cook in a **potli** as described in the "Mutanjan Pulao", one of the greatest pulao recipes of India.

The Lucknowis, Awadhis and Hyderabadis from whom we get our old-world Pulaos and Biryanis used a ghastly attar or aromatic essence — ittar — called Kewra — made from the screw pine. I cannot stand the smell so I never use it. If any of you want to try it please feel free to splash it on the ready pulao. At a pinch, I prefer to use pink or red rose petals or a little rose water on sweets and in certain pulaos.

Another item included in these old recipes, especially by Kashmiris, Gujaratis and in the Southern Indian peninsula and in Bengal is the use of asafoetida. I almost never use it. Many people like to use mustard, sesame and coconut oils in all their food preparations. Please do not use it to make rice dishes. You may fry what goes into the pulao in these oils — but never ever use them to cook the rice itself. It is always good to use the best basmati rice you can afford along with pure ghee and saffron. If you do not want to use pure ghee, use vanaspati ghee but try not to eliminate the saffron. It gives a unique and distinctive flavour to your food.

1. In former times the onions were fried and then the rice was washed and fried along with the onions so that the grains would be separate when cooked. If using the rice cooker there is no need to do this. The rice automatically cooks well if the right amount of water is added. Just toss in the deep fried sliced onions.

2. (a) In the rice cooker you add one and a half times the quantity of water as compared to rice. If you take one measure of rice, whatever you are used to, a cup, a glass, a measuring cup, an empty jam or fruit can, you have to put one and a half measures of water.

    (b) If you are using very old basmati rice use your discretion as regards water. You may need more water.

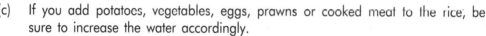

(c) If you add potatoes, vegetables, eggs, prawns or cooked meat to the rice, be sure to increase the water accordingly.

3. In olden times, hours were taken to cook the meat for pulaos and biryanis. Coal sigris were used. Today's young mostly live in modern flats where there is no opportunity to cook on coal. Most people use gas, as a quick, easy and non-smelly medium to cook on. Coal emits smoke and smell and except for the very poor or large caterers, coal is very rarely used in the cities.

4. The pressure cooker is a great boon to modern housewives, many of whom, have to go to work as well as cook and look after household chores and children. The electric rice cooker has further lessened the housewives bane of looking after the rice on an open fire. She had to be constantly alert and on the watch that the water did not dry up or the rice burn up. Now all she has to do is put all the necessary items in the rice cooker and put on the switch. The cooker will automatically go off when the rice is done.

5. Through practice and error, women learn to cook the rice in a pressure cooker. Although edible, it cannot be controlled like the rice in the electric cooker, which comes out in top quality — neither soft nor hard if proper water is added to the rice.

When you open the pulao or biryani vessel an indescribable, heavenly aroma should assail your nostrils, should make your taste buds water and should pervade the atmosphere and make it sublime.

If you are a new bride or just indifferent towards cooking don't lose heart. After a couple of tries you will definitely climb the ladder to success.

If you are an avid cook, use this book lovingly. Add whatever you wish to the recipes, subtract what you dislike. Use ghee, oil, chillies and peppercorns as you wish according to your family taste. There are many pulaos, which are my own personal recipes. One of them is the "Stuffed Snake Gourd Pulao". Try out new ideas; don't stick only to simple mutton or chicken cooked with rice. Go all the way — be adventurous and use these pulaos as a stepping-stone to create your own recipes. A little courage will turn you into a fantastic cook. So here's to happy eating.

THE MAJOR INGREDIENTS FOR PULAOS AND BIRYANIS

Basically, the ingredients are few; the methods of cooking are many. The spices are also mainly the same. It is how and in what quantity that you use them and what accompaniments are added to the dish itself that distinguishes the many rich and varied rice dishes.

Cookery was on a par with music, poetry, singing and painting in the courts of the Lucknowi Nawabs and Rajas, at the Awadhi court of Muzaffer Ali and then later in Hyderabad under the Asafjahis. Chefs from different "Nawabi Khandaans" vied with each other in presenting novel ways with mutton, chicken, fish and shikar birds such as the mallard (batak), partridge (teetar) and quails (bater). Pride was taken in cooking shikar animals such as the hare (khargosh) and the wild boar (soovar). The skin of the latter with a thin layering of fat was highly prized.

THE BASIC ITEMS NECESSARY IN YOUR PANTRY

I would suggest, that you keep atleast 200 gms each of the various items I have listed below. If this is not convenient for whatever reason, you will have to go to the bazaar and shop for them every time you wish to make any of these tasty dishes and ultimately buying in very small quantities will cost you more in the long run.

FOR THE RICE

Saffron
Best quality basmati rice
Pure ghee

FOR THE BODY OF THE PULAOS AND BIRYANIS

Chicken
Eggs
Fish
Mutton
Vegetables

FOR THE SPICES

1. Allspice (Kababchini)
2. Green Mango powder (Amchoor)
3. Anise (Saunf)
4. Asafoetida (Hing)
5. Bay leaf (Tej Patta)
6. Cardamoms (Elaichi, black, white or green)
7. Carraway seeds
8. Chillies (Green as well as dried) (Marcha or Mirchi)
9. Cinnamon (Taj)
10. Cloves (Lavang)
11. Coriander (Dhana dried seeds; fresh leaves Kothmir)
12. Cumin (Jeera)
13. Curry leaves (Kari Patta; Mitho Limro)
14. Fenugreek (Methi)
15. Garlic (Lasun)
16. Ginger (Adrak)
17. Jaggery (Gur)
18. Mace (Javantri)
19. Mint (Pudina)
20. Mustard (Rai)
21. Nigella (Onion seeds)
22. Nutmeg (Jaiphal)
23. Pomegranate seeds (Dalim seeds)
24. Poppy seeds (Khus Khus)
25. Rose petals — rose essence (gulab ke patte; gulabjal)

26. Star anise (Badiyan)
27. Screwpine essence (Kewra)
28. Silver foil (Chandi ka vark)
29. Sugar (Chini)
30. Tamarind (Imli)
31. Turmeric (Haldi)
32. Vinegar (Sugarcane sirka)

NUTS AND DRIED FRUITS

1. Almonds (Badam)
2. Apricots (Jardaloo — Khubani)
3. Cashewnuts (Kaju)
4. Chironji — Charoli
5. Coconut (Nariyel; Dried Kopra)
6. Dates (Khajur)
7. Raisins (Kismis)
8. Pistachios (Pista)
9. Walnuts (Akhrot)

DAIRY PRODUCTS MUST ALL BE BOUGHT FRESH

1. Butter
2. Curd
3. Ghee
4. Lassi
5. Mawa
6. Milk
7. Paneer
8. Cream

A FEW SIMPLE HINTS FOR COOKING THE RICE

1. Always wash the rice twice or thrice.

2. Always remember to add proper amount of water — **one part rice to one and a half parts water.**

3. In a rice cooker, **to one measure of rice add 1½ measures of water.**

4. If using old and very superior rice you may need a little more water.

5. If you like you can fry the onions and rice and spices and then place them in the rice cooker with water and salt. If pressed for time, add everything at once and cook the rice in the rice cooker. It's a matter of personal choice and a question of time.

6. In order to seal the vessel with dough, prepare a mixture of half kilogramme of wheat flour with one and a half cups of water. Knead well and form into a long roll. Take one end of the roll and place it between the lid and the vessel's rim and close the vessel totally so that no steam can escape from the vessel. The contents will then be cooked in the steam created in the vessel. Do not try this in an electric rice cooker.

7. Saffron must be lightly heated over an iron tava or non-stick frying pan. Make a little bundle of your kitchen napkin and shift the thin saffron stamens from side to side for three minutes. Crumble into half a cup of hot milk or half a cup of hot water, I crumble mine directly into the rice and water in the rice cooker.

HYDERABAD

In the 16th century, one of the most splendid cities in India was Golconda. There came a time when this royal city became a morass of disasters. From being a scintillating, rich city full of poets, nautch girls, historians, scholars, jewellers, epicureans and gourmands, it denigrated to an overcrowded city, wherein water was difficult to find, diseases multiplied, until the dreaded plague emerged as the last straw.

Sultan Mohammed Quli Qutub Shah decided to establish a new city in the plains, where the rich and the aristocrats had mango gardens and water ponds. A city without ramparts and gigantic walls. He called it Hyderabad after a courtesan he was madly in love with – a Hindu lady called Bhagmati. So enamoured of her was he that he finally married her and gave her an official title Hyder Mahal.

Mohammed Quli was an extremely swashbuckling character. He was an hedonistic ruler, a poet, an epicurean and a mystic who saw no difference between a Mohammedan and a Hindu. He wished for a secular State wherein all people lived in harmony. Silver, Gold and Pearls became very important items of export. Hyderabad teemed with merchants and rich businessmen. The art of jewellery-making in pearls, emeralds and gold reached a new high. Cuisine reached a new peak and the Master Chefs of grand lords would vie with one another, try to outdo each other, in the tables they set.

The last flamboyant Sultan called lovingly "Tane Shah" was defeated by Aurangzeb's army and a new Governor was appointed. His name was Kamruddin "Nizam Ul Mulk". Later on, he was given the title "Asaf Jah". His dynasty ruled Hyderabad for well over 200 years. The last Nizam, one of the richest men on earth, ruled till 1947. Needless to say the Nizams carried on the tradition of the Qutub Shahis by building luxurious palaces, wearing sensationally expensive clothes, patronising artists and amassing vast fortunes in pearls and gold.

AWADH

Lucknow was the most important traditional part of Awadh. Nawab Asaf-Ud-Daulah created Lucknow from the village it was and constructed large buildings such as the one, which was taken over by the British Residency, the Rumi Darwaza and the great Imambara. His grandson Wajid Ali Shah built the Kaiserbaug.

The Nawabs had a magnificent court, with poets, scholars and noblemen vying for positions amidst the opulence, mehfils and grand dastarkhwans, so that it put to shame the conservative court of Delhi. The "Zaiqa", taste that they left behind in their cuisine, their clothes sense, their music, their songs, their nautch girls is alive even today several hundred years later.

Wajid Ali Shah was deposed by the British in 1856. He was a hedonist in every sense of the word. He lived for pleasure and beauty and was so involved in his musicians and his dancing girls, his cooks or rakabdars, his artists and his designers that he never even realized the British were after his kingdom until he was dispossessed of it. The brilliance, exoticism, graciousness, lavishness, effulgence which the kingdom of Awadh had displayed, never ever, shone again over an India on which the sun arose. But dim rays still exist of the lost grandeur and faded embers of the golden court shine through in the lifestyles of his descendants and relatives in their everyday life and their kitchens, which still stir out exquisite cuisine. Items such as "Jungli Raan", Rizala, Mutton Khurma, Nehari, Pasande, Tunde Kabab, Murg Musallam, Teetar, Macchli Zamin Doz, Khatti Macchli, Dum Lucknowi Biryani, Zarda and Ananas ka Muzaffar are enjoyed even today.

In Wajid Ali Shah's times, spring or Vasant was celebrated in style. Barge processions were taken out on the Gomti river and the revellers were all dressed in yellow to be one with spring, which brought out millions of yellow plants of sarson or mustard. The men and women would dance on the boat decks in gay abandon. All that is left today are the rippling waters of the Gomti, both its banks lapping the fields of yellow mustard.

KHOJA BIRYANI KACHIWALI

FOR THE RICE

2	gms. saffron
500	gms. basmati rice
3	large brown cardamoms
3	star anise
10	black peppercorns
4	bay leaves
2"	piece cinnamon

Pinch of biryani colour
Salt
Pure ghee

FOR THE MUTTON

1	kg. mutton leg pieces
300	gms. tomatoes
300	gms. sliced deep fried onions
200	gms. potatoes skinned and cubed
300	gms. curd

2	tbsps. garam masala	
1	tbsp. chilli powder	
1	tbsp. cumin seeds	
2"	piece cinnamon broken into 3 pieces	Keep whole
4	crushed green cardamoms	
1½	tsps. shahjeera seeds	
1	tsp. carraway seeds	

12	dried apricots

Juice of 2 sour limes
Salt
Pure ghee

FOR THE GROUND MASALA

8	green chillies deseeded	
2	cups of washed fresh coriander leaves	Grind in a little water
2"	piece fresh ginger sliced	
15	cloves of garlic	
10	black peppercorns	

• Wash the mutton and marinate it in the chilli powder, ground masala, curd, lime juice and chopped tomatoes for almost 5 hours or preferably overnight in a cool place.

• The next day fry the sliced onions to a crisp golden brown colour. Remove and set aside. In the same ghee fry the potato cubes to a golden colour. Salt them and set aside.

• Take a heavy bottomed biryani vessel and if possible cover the outside bottom with a layer of water and ash. Heavily grease the vessel from inside with ghee and place 1½ cups of ghee in the vessel and put on a medium heat. When the ghee becomes hot put in the whole spices and fry for 2 minutes. Then add the mutton and fry for 10 minutes on a medium flame. Add the dried apricots.

• Wash the rice twice. Place a vessel on the fire with 1 cup of ghee. Add the cardamoms, star anise, cinnamon, black peppercorns, and bay leaves. Stir for 2 minutes and add the rice and salt. Remove from the fire and place one third over the fried mutton. Make layers of rice, potatoes and fried onions. Mix the colour in ½ cup of water and sprinkle over the rice. Heat the saffron and crumble it directly over the rice. Add 4 cups of water and cover the vessel with a tight lid. Take fresh dough and seal the vessel's rim with that of the lid. Place an iron tava on a medium flame and put the biryani vessel on top of it. Cook for 2½ hours.

• If you wish you can add dhungar to it. Heat some coals and place them in a katori. Add 1 tablespoon pure ghee to the coals and quickly place the vessel on top of the rice and cover it with a lid. When you open the vessel after the meat and rice is cooked a heady aroma will surround you and the dining room.

Accompaniments:

Chicken gravy

Dahi-pineapple raita

Sesame and raw mango chutney

Pink agar-agar dessert decorated with pink rose petals

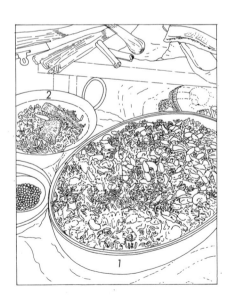

Cover Photograph:

1. *Maplah Meen Biryani*
2. *Portion of the prepared biryani*

DUM PUKHT LUCKNOWI BIRYANI

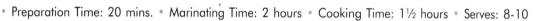

• Preparation Time: 20 mins. • Marinating Time: 2 hours • Cooking Time: 1½ hours • Serves: 8-10

FOR THE RICE

2   gms. saffron
750 gms. basmati rice
4   bay leaves
4   cloves
Salt
Pure ghee

FOR THE MUTTON

1250 gms. mutton pieces (chops, neck portion and leg pieces)
2   tbsps. ginger garlic paste
400 gms. curd
½   litre balai or barhi if available (This is milk from a freshly delivered cow or buffalo and highly valued in northern India)
1   tsp. chilli powder
2   large onions sliced and deep fried
Salt
Pure ghee

FOR THE GROUND MASALA

6   green cardamom seeds
1   small piece of nutmeg
6   cloves
5   mace flowers   } Grind in a little water
2"   piece cinnamon
1   tsp. shahjeera
1   tbsp. coriander seeds
100 gms. almonds, blanched, ground reserve separately

• Wash the meat twice and marinate in the ginger-garlic paste and salt and keep aside for 2 hours.

• Grind the garam masala. Grind the almonds separately and keep aside.

• Deep fry the sliced onions in pure ghee and set aside.

• Boil the meat in plenty of water till the meat is tender. If you do not use the pressure cooker it will take 2 hours. Remove the tender meat pieces. Strain the mutton soup and keep aside.

• Heat 1 cup of ghee in a heavy bottomed pan. Fry the garam masala, ground almonds, chilli powder, and the meat. Add curd and cook till dry.

• Place an iron fry pan or tava with ½ a cup of pure ghee on the fire. Put the mutton pieces in the hot ghee and fry until crisp on both sides. Replace the mutton pieces into the same pan it was cooked with the curd and masala gravy.

• Wash the rice and soak it well for ½ an hour. Wash twice and drain. Fry the rice in ½ a cup of ghee along with the bay leaves, cloves and salt. Then place the rice over the cooked meat. Measure the amount of the strained mutton soup you will need to cook the rice and using your own judgement carefully strain the "barhi" or "balai" into the soup stock and add it to the vessel. Heat the saffron and crumble it directly on to the rice. Check again for salt and for the right amount of soup stock you need. Cover with a tight fitting lid. Take fresh dough and seal the lid and the vessel together. Place on a tava over a medium flame for atleast an hour.

- In northern India, cooks use a lot of sweet attar and kewra essence. I can't stand either of them. Use them at your discretion. Use rose essence if you like on the rice.

- Remove the biryani after 12-15 minutes once you have removed it from the fire. Decorate with plenty of fried onions.

Accompaniments:

Mutton kababs

A fancy salad of apples, peaches and grapes

Raw papaya chutney

Cone Kulfi with saffron falooda strings

HYDERABADI BIRYANI

- Preparation Time: 40 mins. • Marinating Time: 2-6 hours • Cooking Time: 2-2½ hours
- Serves: 15

There is not much difference between the Lucknowi, Awadhi and Hyderabadi biryanis. The last two pulaos, unlike the Moghlai ones use green chillies, which is an influence gained from the Hindu cuisine, which existed, and exits in the region. The land was captured but the Muslim hearts were in turn captured by the conquered ones' cuisine. When I normally recommend leg mutton with nali for my biryani recipes, the Lucknowi one includes, chop meat, meat from the neck which is purdah, thin and soft, and leg meat. The Hyderabadi biryani uses portions of meat from the shoulder which again is thin and soft, nali with meat on it and pieces from the shoulder.

As regards the rice for these biryanis, no shortcut should be taken — use the best possible rice you can afford.

FOR THE RICE

2	gms. saffron
1	kg. basmati rice
2	cups hot milk
6-8	crushed green cardamoms
4	(1") pieces of cinnamon
5	bay leaves
1	tsp. fennel seeds
1	tsp. carraway seeds

Salt
Pure ghee

FOR THE MUTTON

1500	gms. mutton (from the leg, shoulder and chops)
500	gms. thick curd
2	tbsps. ginger-garlic paste
1	tbsp. red chilli powder (optional)
4	large sour limes — juice removed
3"	piece raw papaya finely ground

Pure ghee

FOR THE FRIED ONIONS

8	onions skinned and sliced

- Wash the mutton twice and marinate in the ginger-garlic paste, papaya paste, lime juice, curd, chilli powder and salt. The papaya, sour lime and curd will soften the tissues of the meat. All three emit a good taste and are the best amongst the many tenderizing agents. Keep aside for 2 to 6 hours.

- Take a karhai half filled with vanaspati ghee. Heat it. Crush the raw, fine onion slices and deep fry till golden brown. Sprinkle a pinch of garam masala. This is known as "birista". Crush the onions on a grinding stone and mix into the meat.

- Grind the masala for the meat with ½ cup of water. Use more if needed. When it is soft and buttery, apply it to the marinating meat. Wash the grinding stone or mixie with ½ cup of water and add that to the meat also. Mix well and set aside.

- Take a very heavy biryani vessel. If you are going to cook on coal, spread a layer of water and ash on the outside bottom of the vessel. If you are going to cook on gas you will have to keep checking that your mutton does not stick to the centre of the vessel.

GROUND MASALA FOR THE MUTTON

4	star anise	
1½	tbsps. shahjeera	
1	tbsp. carraway seeds	
6	green cardamom seeds only	
15-20	peppercorns	
2"	piece cinnamon	Grind in water
6	cloves	
6	onions finely sliced	
6	green chillies — deseeded	
1	bunch of fresh coriander cleaned, washed and finely chopped	
1	cup mint — leaves only cleaned, finely chopped	
5	mace flowers	

EXTRAS

5   leaves of silver vark

- Place 2 cups of pure ghee into the biryani vessel. Place on medium heat. Add the mutton pieces to the hot ghee and stir till nicely red and fried. Add all the marinating liquid and lower the flame. Stir well and cover with a deep lid so you can fill it with the water. Every 15-20 minutes open the vessel, stir and add the extra water on the lid. Indian mutton being tough, inspite of the tenderizing agents it may take 2 hours or a little more.

- When the meat has become tender and about 2 cups of gravy is left, take a large, wide mouthed vessel and fill it half way up with water. Wash the rice twice. Put in the boiling water along with salt, green cardamoms, cinnamon, bay leaves, fennel seeds, carraway seeds and ½ to 1 cup of pure ghee. Cook the rice till it is three quarters cooked. Drain and spread it out on a large thala.

- Heat the saffron on a tava till crisp. Keep shaking it from side to side with a rolled up piece of muslin. Please do not burn it. Heat the milk and crumble the saffron into it. Sprinkle it over the rice and mix well. Stir the meat gently in the vessel and place the boiled rice on top of it. Spread it and make it level. Then cover it with a tight lid. Take dough, roll it into a long coil and tie it tightly around the rims of the lid and the vessel to make the vessel air tight. Take a large iron tava and place it on a medium flame and place the biryani vessel on top of it for 30 to 40 minutes. When the time is up remove the vessel from the fire. Do not open it for 12-15 minutes. Open and serve the biryani with a quarter plate on to a silver salver. Cover with the silver vark.

Accompaniments:

Hot spicy dal

A luscious mutton dish with narrow raw carrots, raisins and tomatoes

Chilli pickle

A dessert of pounded almonds and rice cooked in creamy milk

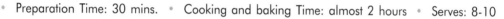

CHILMAN BIRYANI

• Preparation Time: 30 mins. • Cooking and baking Time: almost 2 hours • Serves: 8-10

FOR THE RICE

2 gms. saffron
400 gms. basmati rice
4 bay leaves
5 bara elcha (large cardamom)
3 green cardamom
10 black peppercorns
2 large onions sliced and fried
Salt
Ghee

FOR THE MUTTON

800 gms. mutton (chunks with nali)
3 large onions fried and crushed
1¼ tbsps. ginger-garlic paste
10 kashmiri chillies deseeded
1 tbsp. coriander seeds broiled
½ tbsp. cumin seeds broiled
½ tbsp. fennel seeds broiled
½ tbsp. black peppercorns broiled
1" piece cinnamon
½ tsp. green cardamom seeds
6 cloves
4 mace flowers

} Grind with a little water

Salt
Ghee

FOR THE PUFF PASTRY

250 gms. maida
250 gms. butter or ghee
1 tsp. baking powder
Salt to taste
Water as necessary
Aluminium, terracotta or pyrex moulds for the biryani

• Cook the rice in two parts. Cook one with the saffron and the other with the whole spices and fried onions in a rice cooker. Add salt and to each portion half a tablespoon of ghee.

• Cook the mutton in the pressure cooker. Take a cup of ghee in a vessel and add the mutton, salt, ginger-garlic and cook till the meat is red. Add the ground masala and lower the flame and stir the mutton for 5 minutes till it is well covered with the masala. Add water and cook till the mutton is tender and if any soup is left dry it up.

• Make the puff pastry in a thali. Put the flour and baking powder and mix both. Sprinkle some salt over the flour and make a shallow depression in the centre. Put in the butter or ghee and mix lightly and add a sprinkle of water till you have a nice soft dough.

• Place layers of rice and meat in the small baking dishes. Place little dollops of crushed onions on the top of each little vessel. Then cover the vessels with a pastry layer on top. Make a slightly thick dough and apply round the edges of the moulds to see that the biryani is totally sealed. Cover the pastry tops with little decorations of leaves, vines, flowers, buds or fruit. Place in a hot oven at 350°F until the top cooks to a golden brown.

Accompaniments:

Dhansak Dal

Tomato and apple chutney

A dish of mince

A green cucumber, avocado and lettuce salad

Mango Ice-cream for dessert

KASHMIRI BHUNE (ROASTED) GOSHT KI BIRYANI

• Preparation Time: 15 mins. • Marinating Time: 2 hours • Cooking Time: 2¼ hours
• Serves: 10-12

FOR THE RICE

900 gms. basmati rice
Salt
Pure ghee

FOR THE MUTTON

2 kgs. mutton (leg chunks with nali)
500 gms. curd
225 gms. mawa
2" piece of ginger freshly ground
2 tbsps. garam masala powder
2 tbsps. kashmiri chilli powder
1½ tbsps. turmeric powder
1 tbsp. dried ginger powder
1 tbsp. crushed anise seeds
7 crushed cloves
8 crushed green cardamoms
6 crushed mace flowers
2" cinnamon broken into bits
2 tbsps. broiled and crushed shahjeera
1 tsp. asafoetida
Salt
Pure ghee

FOR DECORATION AND EXTRAS

500 gms. potatoes skinned and cut into big cubes and deep fried till golden brown
150 gms. sliced almonds
100 gms. raisins

Accompaniments:

Boondi Raita

Crisp green leafed salad with peeled orange segments

A gravied chicken dish

Almond and Rice Kheer

• Wash the meat twice and marinate it in the salt and fresh-ground ginger for half an hour. Then add the garam masala, chilli powder, turmeric powder and curd and allow to rest for 2 hours atleast.

• Take a large biryani vessel. Add 1½ cups of pure ghee to it. Place on medium heat and add the whole spices such as cloves, cinnamon, cardamoms, mace, anise seeds and dried ginger powder and cook over low heat for 5 minutes. Add the marinated meat along with all its gravy and the asafoetida. Increase the flame to medium heat and with a heavy iron ladle keep frying the meat non-stop for 15 minutes. As soon as the gravy dries up, add more water and fry the meat, stirring continuously. When the mutton turns a red colour, add sufficient water to tenderize it and cook over a medium flame till the mutton gets soft. Pour sufficient water for the rice to cook in the mutton soup and add rice. Sprinkle the crushed shahjeera and taste for salt.

• Heat the saffron and soak it in half a cup of hot water and add it to the rice.

• Dilute the mawa in ¼ cup of hot water and pour it over the rice. Cover with a tight lid and seal with dough.

• Place over an iron tava for about an hour. Rest the pulao for 10 minutes.

• Meanwhile fry the boiled, skinned, sliced almonds and raisins in 1 cup of pure ghee. When ready to serve the rice, open the vessel and pour the ghee over the rice and sprinkle the almonds and raisins over it also. Take the narrow end of the ladle and gently mix the biryani and serve in a salver decorated with fresh mint and fruits.

A MAD HATTER'S PULAO OF BONELESS MEAT AND GREENS

• Preparation Time: 25 mins. • Marinating Time: 1 hour • Cooking Time: 50 mins.
• Serves: 6-8

FOR THE RICE
400 gms. basmati rice
1 tsp. carraway seeds
Salt
Ghee

FOR THE MEAT
1 bunch dill or suva bhaji washed and chopped
3 bunches palak bhaji washed and chopped
3 bunches chowlai bhaji washed and chopped
2 bunches fresh coriander washed and chopped
1 kg. mutton cut into one inch pieces
2 tbsps. ginger-garlic paste
Ghee

FOR THE MASALA
2" piece cinnamon
4 cloves
1 tbsp. cumin seeds   } Grind with a little water
10 large cloves garlic
8 green chillies deseeded
10 black peppercorns
3 sour limes squeezed for juice
2 tbsps. sugar
Salt

FOR THE ONION BAGHAR
3 onions, sliced and deep fried set aside
3 onions finely chopped
2 whole red kashmiri chillies
1 tsp. fennel seeds
1 tsp. turmeric

• Cook the rice in your rice cooker along with the carraway seeds, salt and ghee.

• Wash the bhaji or different types of spinach well and chop very finely. Set aside.

• Apply the ginger-garlic paste and salt to the mutton. When the ground masala is ready, marinate the meat in it for at least an hour.

• Chop the onions finely and place in a vessel along with 3 tablespoons of ghee. When the onion becomes soft, add the mutton and stir for 5 to 8 minutes in its own juice, add the chopped bhajis and lower the heat stirring vigorously. Taste for salt. Place the mixture into a pressure cooker, add 2-3 cups of water and cook for 15 minutes after the whistle on a low flame. The mutton should be tender when you open the cooker. Remove the mutton and spinach into a flat bottomed vessel; and allow the water to evaporate till you get a thick mixture with the ghee floating on top.

• Take a vessel and make layers of the meat and rice and cover tightly and place on an iron tava and allow to heat for 20 minutes.

Accompaniments:
Pomegranate Raita
Hot Mango Chutney
Masala Murgh
Sweet Kulfi with Sev

PULAO MUTANJAN

• Preparation Time: 40 mins. • Marinating Time: 2 hours • Cooking Time: 2½ hours • Serves: 10

This pulao is not easy to make. Great importance is placed on the soup that has to be cooked so that the rice can be cooked first in an aromatic fashion and simultaneously the mutton has to be cooked till tender. So we have two functions created in one action. Of course, there are many ways of making this pulao without the aromatic "Potli" soup but somehow I find my recipe the most suitable. Many North Indian cooks use the "Mind blowing attar KEWRA" in their pulaos. I don't. I prefer to use fresh pink rose petals and rose water or failing it a wee bit of rose essence diluted in water.

The beauty and sophistication of this dish, its aroma and its subtle blends of sweet, sour, spicy and flowery perfumes are not to be found in any other pulao in Hindustan or Pakistan.

This royal recipe is pure Moghlai: one could go so far as to say that it was created to taste and please the palates of Babur's family, friends and descendants. It is said that he missed the sights and smells of his dear homeland Ferghana and often fell into a homesick reverie. Throughout Moghul cooking runs a recurring thread of Persian nostalgia.

The first time I saw this pulao being cooked was in my paternal grandmother Cooverbai's kitchen. My aunt Shirin Boga, who had been born and brought up in Rawalpindi had come to us on a visit from London. We never called the pulao "Mutanjan". To us it was known as the great "Potli No Pulao" because whilst making the Yakhni, Shirin used to tie all the whole garam masala into a square of muslin, tie up the four corners to make a parcel, with a long string which well extended beyond the rim of the vessel and could be pulled up and down to squeeze maximum flavours from the whole spices whilst the soup bubbled and boiled. The long string also saved the fingertips from scalding, whilst drawing up the "Potli" which was eventually discarded.

STAGE – I

FOR THE POTLI SOUP

1200 gms. best of mutton cut into 1½" cubes along with nali pieces from the leg
2   tbsps. ginger-garlic paste
2   large onions fried in pure ghee
Salt

• Wash the mutton well and marinate in salt and the ginger-garlic paste for 2 hours.

• Cook the onions in a large heavy bottomed vessel and when they become golden in colour close the stove.

A piece of muslin 10" × 10" square.
On it place whole spices such as:

8	green cardamoms crushed whole
6	cloves lightly bruised
24	black peppercorns thumped in a brown paper bag
2-3	pieces of cinnamon 3" in all.
4-5	mace flowers
3-4	star anise seeds
1	tbsp. fennel seeds bruised
1	tbsp. cumin seeds bruised
1	tbsp. coriander seeds bruised
4	bay leaves

Place all this in the muslin and tie the 4 corners with a long string till the parcel is completely sealed and none of the spice will leak out.

- Add the mutton to the fried onions and mix well. Add 10 cups of water into the pan and lower the "Potli" of spices to the pan. Take care to keep the long string below a heavy weight. Keep cooking the soup till the meat is tender. Keep dipping the potli up and down periodically to give the spices a chance to evict their essence. This process will take 2 to 3 hours as Indian mutton is tough. When done, remove the potli from the soup and separate the cooked meat from the soup.

STAGE – II

To prepare the sweet and sour portion of the pulao we will need:
Juice of 3 sour limes

1	cup of honey
2	cups of sugar
4	cups of water

- Boil the water with the sugar and make a 1 strand syrup. Add the lime juice. Remove any scum which floats up on top, add the honey, mix well, cool and set aside.

STAGE – III

250	gms. of fine mutton mince
1	onion finely chopped
6	green chillies deseeded and chopped
	Ghee
4	tbsps. fresh coriander finely minced
3	tsps. minced fresh mint
3	tsps. minced fresh ginger
2	tsps. minced fresh garlic
1	tbsp. garam masala
4	tbsps. gram dal soaked overnight and ground to a paste with a pinch of salt OR
7	slices stale or one day old bread soaked and crushed fine along with 2 well beaten eggs

- Mix all the ingredients and taste for salt. Form small little balls and deep fry in hot ghee. Cool.

STAGE – IV

200	gms. thick curd
4	red kashmiri chillies broken into bits
1	tbsp. powdered fennel seeds
1	tbsp. powdered coriander seeds
1	tbsp. garam masala
1	tbsp. black pepper powder
¾	teacup pure ghee

- Place a vessel on the fire and when the ghee is moderately hot fry the dry chilli bits till they are soft and pulpy. Lower the heat, mix the chillies vigorously and add the curd, fennel, coriander, pepper powder and the garam masala. Add the soft cooked meat and gently stir over a low fire for 5 minutes. Cool.

STAGE – V

2-3	gms. saffron
700	gms. Old Sadhu Chhaap basmati rice
6	cups of "Yakhni" soup
4	bay leaves
½	cup ghee
Salt	

- Wash the rice thrice and cook in the saffron and six cups of yakhni. Add the ghee, bay leaves and salt to taste and cook till the rice is almost done in a rice cooker or out on a stove.

  Gently take a spatula and separate the rice grains. Cool.

STAGE – VI

50	gms. almonds, blanched sliced and deep fried
50	gms. pistachios skinned, sliced and deep fried
100	gms. seedless raisins washed and deep fried
1	cup pink rose petals
2	onions halved sliced and deep fried

Few drops [8] rose essence (optional)
Fried potato cubes

- Take a large biryani dekchi. Sprinkle a little ghee on its base. Place a layer of rice at the bottom and top it with a layer of cooked meat. Top with rice, sprinkle with the honey, sugar and lemon sauce, the fried baby kababs, raisins, almonds, pistachios and rose petals. Layer in this way till you have used up all your material. Keep raisins, nuts and rose petals for the top. Cover tightly with foil or a lid over which you have patched wet dough. Leave on dum for 15-20 minutes on a large tava over medium flame.

Accompaniments:

Onion kachumber
A Chicken masala dish
Lightly sautéed cabbage
Rawa (soji) with sliced almonds

DELICIOUS GREEN MUTTON BIRYANI

• Preparation + Marinating Time: 3½ hours • Cooking Time: 3½-4 hours • Serves: 10-12

FOR THE RICE

4	gms. saffron
1	kg. basmati rice
6	crushed green cardamoms

Pure ghee

FOR THE MUTTON

1500	gms. mutton (leg chunks with nali)
2	tbsps. ginger-garlic paste
3″ × 3″	piece of raw papaya with the skin ground finely

FOR THE MASALA

2	bunches coriander chopped
½	bunch fresh mint chopped
20	green chillies deseeded
3″	piece cinnamon broken into bits
7	cloves
25	black peppercorns
6	green cardamoms seeds
2	mace flowers
3	star anise
1	tbsp. shahjeera
1	tbsp. fennel
1	kg. thick full cream yoghurt

Grind finely in half to one cup of water

800	gms. onions, peeled, sliced, fried
500	gms. potatoes, peeled, cubed, fried

Salt, Ghee/Oil

• Marinate the mutton in salt, ginger-garlic and the raw papaya paste. Set aside till the masala is ground. Grind the masala very fine and mix into the mutton and allow to marinate for atleast 2 hours. Reserve the water with which you wash the mixie or grinding stone.

• Take a heavy bottomed biryani vessel and grease the bottom and sides with ghee.

• Heat a large vessel, half filled with water. Add salt and the washed rice. Allow to parboil and drain the rice in a large colander. Cool in a thali.

• Whisk the yoghurt and add it to the marinating mutton and keep it for an extra hour.

• Place some of the mutton on the bottom of the greased vessel. Place a layer of rice and fried onions and potatoes on it. Cover again with a layer of mutton then rice and the fried onions and potatoes. Cover with a heavy lid and seal the vessel with dough. Place on a tava over medium heat for 3½ to 4 hours.

Accompaniments:

Potato curry

Masala Chicken

Salad of cucumbers, tomatoes, onions, green chillies and lime juice

Coconut-cream Ice-cream

GREEN MUTTON BIRYANI THE PRESSURE COOKER WAY

All the items remain the same. Only the method is different.

Place the fried onions at the bottom of a pressure cooker. When hot, add two tablespoons ghee and the mutton which has been marinated along with the ghee. Add 2 cups of water. and pressure-cook for 20 minutes.

Open the cooker, check the liquid and if it is not enough to cook the rice, add some water. Place the washed rice on top of the cooked mutton. Sprinkle with salt. Add dollops of pure ghee and shut the cooker. Place over a medium flame and wait for one whistle. Cook over a low flame for 10 minutes and serve in a silver salver covered with the fried potatoes.

SEVIYON (VERMICELLI) KA MASALEDAR PULAO/BIRYANI

This is a totally new type of pulao. I have come across it in only two books so far. One is the fascinating work of Digvijay Singh on the "Cooking Delights of the Maharajas". It is an outstanding and totally original work. The other is the beautifully photographed book by Pratibha Kiran called "Hyderabadi Cuisine".

The difficult part of this unique recipe is the handling and cooking of the vermicelli. Mostly different communities cook it in milk, sugar and nuts. Parsis have to do the difficult thing – they fry the vermicelli golden brown, remove the ghee and cook it soft by adding a little sugar water at a time till it becomes sweet, soft and tender. No mean feat. Very few people have the patience of cooking vermicelli over a stove.

KATY DALAL'S VERMICELLI PULAO

- Preparation Time: 25 mins. • Marinating Time: 1 hour • Cooking Time: 1 hour
- Serves: 6-8

FOR THE VERMICELLI

200 gms. vermicelli
One pinch mace powder
One pinch cardamom powder
Sprinkle fine salt
Pure ghee

FOR THE MUTTON

600 gms. leg mutton (boneless cut into 1½" chunks)
200 gms. curd
4 onions deep fried and ground
Salt
Pure ghee

- Wash the mutton twice. Salt it. Whisk the curd and add it to the mutton. Crush the fried onions on a grinding stone or mixie and also add it to the mutton. Mix well and set aside for atleast an hour.

- Once the masala is finely ground, retain the water with which you wash the grinding stone or mixie.

- Heat 2 tablespoons of pure ghee in a pressure cooker. When hot, fry the masala till almost red and then add the meat and lower the flame. Mix well and taste for salt and then cook till tender with 4 cups of water.

1. Pulao Mutanjan
2. Sautéed Cabbage
3. Kachumber
4. Rawa with sliced almonds

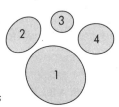

MASALA FOR THE MUTTON

10	red chillies deseeded
2	green chillies deseeded
15	black peppercorns
2"	stick cinnamon
5	cloves
4	green cardamoms seeds only
3	star anise
½	tbsp. cumin seeds broiled
½	tbsp. coriander seeds broiled
1	cup coriander chopped

Grind fine with ¼ cup water

FOR THE DECORATION

½	teacup fried raisins
¼	teacup pistachio slices
3	sheets silver vark

• Place ghee in a karhai and break the vermicelli into 2" pieces. When the ghee is hot, fry the vermicelli to golden brown in small batches. Drain in a colander and sprinkle with the mace, cardamom powder and fine salt.

• Put all the cooked meat in an electric cooker. Measure the soup in cups. You should have atleast 2½ cups of soup left. Place the soup, as much as required, onto the mutton. Top with the vermicelli and allow to cook till tender, when the cooker will automatically switch off.

• This pulao should be had as quickly as possible or it will become mushy. Carefully empty into a flat dish and sprinkle with the fried raisins and pistachio slices and cover with the silver vark.

Accompaniments:

Avocado, banana, lettuce, curd and chutney salad
A dish of paneer and mushrooms
Fried brinjal slices
Fresh Strawberry Ice-cream

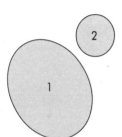

1. *Noor Jehan ka Bemisal Pulao*
2. *Gulab ki Barfi (Rose Barfi)*

KASHMIRI KACHE (RAW) GOSHT KI BIRYANI

• Preparation Time: 15 mins. • Cooking Time: 2¼ hours • Serves: 10-12

FOR THE RICE
800 gms. basmati rice
2 gms. saffron
Salt
Pure ghee

FOR THE MUTTON
1500 gms. mutton (from front legs along with nali)

Place in a potli for yakhni:
50 gms. coriander seeds crushed
20 gms. anise seeds crushed
10 cardamoms crushed
1 tsp. chilli powder
2" piece crushed cinnamon
6 cloves crushed
2" piece crushed fresh ginger
2 tbsps. ground garam masala
1 tsp. asafoetida
Pure ghee

FOR THE DECORATION
100 gms. blanched almonds sliced
100 gms. raisins
1 tbsp. shahjeera broiled and crushed
Pure ghee

• Wash the meat well twice and place it in a large heavy bottomed biryani vessel. Add 3 litres of water and place it on a high flame. Add salt.

• Make a potli for the yakhni. Tie in a large square muslin cloth, the crushed coriander seeds, anise seeds, cardamom seeds, cloves, cinnamon, fresh ginger, garam masala powder and hing. Tie it up with a strong, long white cord which should extend over the vessel and onto the table. Place the potli in the boiling mutton soup and allow the mutton to cook till tender. Keep adding extra water till you have soft mutton and sufficient soup to cook the rice.

• Wash the rice and soak it for 2 to 3 hours.

• Add the chilli powder to the soup, the rice and the extra salt for rice and cook covered tightly till the rice is fluffy and almost done. Heat the saffron and crumble it directly on to the cooking rice. Cover tightly.

• Pour 1½ cups of pure ghee into a small saucepan. Heat it and add the raisins and the almonds last. Make 5 holes in the rice.

• Sprinkle the raisins and almond slices over the biryani and pour the hot ghee down the holes. Cover. After the rice is thoroughly cooked, set aside for 10 minutes and then serve.

• Kewra essence is put in the biryani by grinding the saffron in it. However, many people cannot stand the essence; use your own discretion.

Accompaniments:
Potato and fresh mint raita
Baby onion and tomato salad
A Liver dish
Firni

AYESHA BEGUM KI PYARI BIRYANI (TROTTERS)

• Preparation Time: 25-30 mins. • Cooking Time: 1 hour 25 mins. • Serves: 8

FOR THE RICE

450	gms. basmati rice
3	onions sliced
4	bay leaves
4	crushed green cardamoms
2"	piece cinnamon
8	lightly crushed peppercorns
4	cloves lightly crushed
4	mace flowers
Salt	
Ghee	

FOR THE TROTTERS

18	trotters all front legs, each cut into three
2½	tbsps. ginger-garlic paste
4	large onions finely chopped
Salt	
Ghee	

FOR THE GROUND MASALA

½	dried coconut grated	
12	kashmiri chillies	
12	black peppercorns	
2	(2") pieces cinnamon	
5	cloves	Grind
5	mace flowers	very fine
2	tbsps. coriander seeds broiled	with one cup
2	tbsps. cumin seeds broiled	water
1	tbsp. shahjeera	
1	tsp. dried ginger powder	
1	tsp. dill seeds	

• Wash and clean the trotters well. Wash them 3 times. There should be no hairs sticking to them. Place a pressure cooker on the fire and fill it with 3 litres of water. Apply salt and the ginger-garlic paste to the trotters and put them into the cooker.

• If you wish you can cook the marinated trotters in a large dekchi on a stove or coal fire for 2 to 3 hours till they are soft and the water has reduced considerably.

• Once the trotters are cooked, place them on a high flame until you have about ¾ litre of soup left. Taste for salt.

• Take a large vessel and put in 2 tablespoons of pure ghee. Add the finely chopped onions and cook them till golden in colour. Add the finely ground masala and lower the flame and cook gently for 7 minutes stirring all the time. Add the trotters along with the soup and simmer for 15 minutes till you get a thick, rich soup.

• Wash the rice thrice and set aside. Place the sliced onions and 1½ tablespoons of ghee and cook the onions till soft. Add the cardamoms, cinnamon, peppercorns, cloves, mace and salt and the washed rice and fry for 5 minutes. Place the rice over the trotters and cover with a tight lid, and seal with dough. Place the vessel over a large iron tava, on medium flame for 1½ hours.

Accompaniments:

Sweet yogurt kachumber with coriander, onion and lime juice

Vegetable stew

Stuffed kababs

Pista Kulfi

KHUBANI AUR GOSHT KA LALKAR

• Preparation Time: 15 mins. • Cooking Time: 40 mins. • Serves: 8-10

FOR THE RICE

2	gms. saffron
400	gms. basmati rice
2	onions sliced fried
2"	stick cinnamon
Salt	
Ghee	

FOR THE MUTTON

1	kg. boneless mutton cubes plus nali pieces
1½	tbsps. ginger-garlic paste
450	gms. apricots soaked overnight in water with 2 tablespoons sugar added to it
4	tbsps. seedless raisins washed
4	medium onions finely chopped
300	gms. tomatoes skinned chopped
2	tbsps. garam masala
1	tbsp. chilli powder
1	tbsp. turmeric powder
4	green cardamoms crushed
3	tbsps. sugarcane vinegar
Salt	
Ghee	

• Cook the rice in a rice cooker along with the saffron, spices, salt and ghee.

• Marinate the mutton in salt and ginger-garlic paste.

• Place the chopped onions in a large vessel and cook till golden brown. Add the garam masala, chilli powder, turmeric, cardamoms, tomatoes and fry along with the onions for 2 minutes. Add the mutton and lower the flame and cook in its own juice for 10 to 12 minutes. When the mutton turns red put it in a pressure cooker with 3 to 4 cups of water. Cook on a slow fire for 20 minutes after the whistle. When the mutton is tender, transfer it to a large vessel. Add the soaked apricots and washed raisins and allow the liquid to dry up. Add the vinegar, mix and remove from the fire.

• Layer the pulao, rice — mutton — rice and cover it tightly with foil or a lid sealed with dough. Place on an iron tava on a medium flame for 15 minutes.

Accompaniments:

Akoori of eggs
A lightly spiced vegetable
Curds
Dessert of double-ka-meetha

ANANAS AUR GOSHT KA PULAO

• Preparation Time: 15 mins. • Cooking Time: 50 mins. • Serves: 6-8

FOR THE RICE

450	gms. basmati rice
2	large potatoes cubed
3	large onions sliced and fried
4	bay leaves
4	green cardamoms
2	large black cardamoms
2	tsps. fennel seeds
2	(1") sticks cinnamon
1	pinch saffron colour

Salt
Pure ghee

FOR THE MUTTON

1	kg. leg mutton pieces with nali
2	large onions
1	fresh large pineapple, skinned and eyes cut out OR
1	large canned pineapple slices
2	tbsps. coriander seeds
1	tbsp. fennel seeds
1	tbsp. black peppercorns
1	tbsp. poppy seeds
1	tbsp. sesame seeds
12	dried kashmiri chillies
¼	grated dried coconut
½	cup coriander chopped

} Grind fine with water

Salt
Ghee

Accompaniments:

Mince with potatoes

Hot pickle

Radish salad with cumin powder

Chilli salan

Dudhi Murabba

• Cook the rice in 2 different ways in the rice cooker. First take 250 gms. of rice, the cubed potatoes, ½ the fried onions, 2 bay leaves, 2 green cardamoms, 1 large black cardamom, 1 teaspoon fennel seeds, 1 stick cinnamon, salt and 1 tablespoon ghee. Cook till tender and spread in a thali.

• Cook the second portion of rice, 200 grams, along with the saffron, remaining spices and onions, salt and 1 tablespoon ghee. Cook and cool in a thali to separate the grains.

• Salt the mutton pieces and set aside. Chop the onions, place in a vessel with 3 tablespoons of ghee. Cook till soft. Grind the masala till soft and keep the water with which you wash your grinding stone or mixie. Open the pineapple can, retain the syrup and chop the slices into ½" pieces.

• When the onion is soft, add the mutton pieces and the ground masala, lower the flame and cook without water for 10 minutes. Place in a pressure cooker along with ½ a cup of syrup and 3 cups of water and cook till tender. Open the cooker to check the meat for tenderness; a little gravy should be left.

• Place the rice with the potatoes in a biryani vessel. Smooth the rice and add a layer of all the mutton. Sprinkle some syrup. Place ¾ of the pineapple pieces on top of the mutton and cover with the saffron rice. Top with the left over pineapple pieces. Cover tightly with foil or a lid sealed with dough. Place on an iron griddle over a medium flame for 15 minutes.

• Open only when ready to eat.

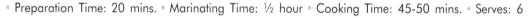

FRESH CHERRY KASHMIRI PULAO

• Preparation Time: 20 mins. • Marinating Time: ½ hour • Cooking Time: 45-50 mins. • Serves: 6

FOR THE RICE

½   gm. saffron
400 gms. basmati rice
1   sliced fried onion
1   tbsp. ghee
Salt

FOR THE MUTTON

1   gm. saffron
900 gms. leg mutton cut into chunks
3   sliced fried onions
400 gms. large dark fresh cherries
1½" ginger freshly ground
Salt
Pure ghee

FOR THE MASALA

1½" cinnamon stick
6   cloves
16 black peppercorns
1   tbsp. shahjeera
4   green cardamoms seeds only
1½ tsps. fennel seeds powdered   } Grind fine
1½ tsps. dried ginger powder
1½ tsps. cumin seeds powdered
¼   tsp. asafoetida
6   dried kashmiri chillies
16 almonds

FOR THE DECORATION

10 fresh cherries with stems

• Wash the mutton twice and marinate in salt and freshly ground ginger for ½ an hour.

• Heat the 3 fried onions and add the mutton and cook over a low fire for 15 minutes. Add the ground masala and keep the water in which you had washed the grinding stone or mixie aside. Simmer in the masala for 5 minutes, stirring well. Add the reserved water. Altogether 3 cups of water must be added to the mutton. Pressure cook till tender.

• Reserve 10 cherries with stems for decoration. Grate the rest with the help of a grater. Throw away the stones. Put the grated cherry mixture into the cooked mutton. Heat 1 gram saffron. Mix into ½ a cup of hot water and add to the mutton and simmer for 10 minutes.

• Cook the rice with the fried onion and the saffron in a rice cooker.

• Sandwich the mutton between two layers of rice in a clean flat-bottomed vessel. Place a large tava on the stove. Then put the vessel on top of it. Make 5 holes in the rice and pour 3 tablespoons melted pure ghee — warm, into them. Seal with foil and allow to cook for a further 15 minutes.

• When serving place the fresh cherries around the vessel.

Accompaniments:

Masala fish
Salad of celery and orange segments
Curd with dill
Apricot chutney
Pista Kulfi

MANGO AND BOTI PULAO

FOR THE RICE

300	gms. basmati rice	
800	gms. good boneless mutton, cut into pieces (botis)	
4	ripe alphonso mangoes skinned and pulped	
2	gms. saffron	
4	lightly pounded green cardamoms	
1"	piece cinnamon broken into two	
8	black peppercorns	
1	tsp. carraway seeds	
2	mace flowers	
1	onion deep fried	
1	tsp. shahjeera	
1	tsp. broken badiyan or star anise	
15	black peppercorns	
1"	piece cinnamon	
6	cloves	
4	mace flowers	
8	red dried kashmiri chillies	
20	almonds	
20	cashewnuts	
1	tbsp. ginger-garlic paste	
400	gms. onions deep fried	
½	cup chopped coriander	
2	tbsps. mint leaves freshly minced	

Grind in a little water for the mutton

Salt
Pure ghee

• Cook the rice in a rice cooker along with the fried onion, cardamoms, cinnamon, peppercorns, carraway seeds and mace flowers. Heat the saffron on a tava and crumble into the rice and water. Cook till tender and cool the rice on a tray.

• Pulp the skinned mangoes and keep in a cool place.

• Wash the meat botis twice. Marinate in salt and the ginger-garlic paste for ½ an hour. Crush the fried onions on a stone quern or mixie and place in a pressure cooker on a low heat. Add the mutton pieces and stir for 7 minutes or so. Raise the heat a little, add ½ a cup of pure ghee, stir for 5 minutes and then add the ground masala. Stir for a full 10 minutes and then add 2½ cups of water and cook till the mutton is tender. Taste for salt.

• Whilst the mutton is cooking, warm the mango pulp over a low flame.

• Place the cooked mutton in a vessel. If much soup is left, dry it.

• Take a high sided pyrex dish, failing which, take a straight sided aluminium vessel. Place half the rice at the base of the dish or vessel. Cover the rice with half the warmed pulp. Then spread all the mutton over the pulp in a thick layer. Cover with the rest of the pulp and then cover with the remaining rice. Scatter the chopped coriander and mint on top and cover with foil and place in an oven at 350°F for 15 minutes. This will allow all the aromas to blend. Serve hot.

COORGI YARCHI (MUTTON) PULAO

• Preparation Time: 15 mins. • Marinating Time: 1 hour • Cooking Time: 2½ hours • Serves: 6-8

As we start going south below the Krishna river, the food gets hotter and hotter as enormous quantities of all different types of chillies are used. Kerala, Malayali, Telugu and Coorgi food comes under this aegis. The beautiful bland, delicate, saffron flavour gives way to a hot, stimulating, energising force. The northerner sometimes has to wipe his eyes and nose and drink copious glasses of water and eat bowlsful of curd whilst doing justice to the chilli food.

The pulaos include red chilli powder as well as green chillies. The Coorgi mutton is no exception. But as a rule Coorgi cuisine does not use curd or yoghurt. It uses a lot of tamarind.

FOR THE RICE

600	gms. basmati rice or any other long grained rice of your choice
2	(1") cinnamon pieces
5	bay leaves
3	large brown cardamoms
1	tsp. kalonji or onion seeds
Salt	
Ghee	

FOR THE MUTTON

1200	gms. leg mutton with nali	
4	large onions finely chopped	
2	tbsps. garlic and ginger paste	
½	bunch chopped fresh coriander leaves	} Grind
2	tbsps. mint	
2	sour limes for juice	
Salt		
Ghee		

• Cook the rice in the rice cooker along with the salt, cinnamon pieces, bay leaves, brown cardamoms, kalonji or onion seeds and 1 tablespoon of pure ghee.

• Wash the mutton pieces well and marinate for atleast 1 hour in the ginger-garlic paste, lime juice and salt.

• Take a large, heavy bottomed vessel. If you are cooking on coal, cover its outside bottom with a layer of ash and water. Place the 4 chopped onions along with 1 cup of pure ghee on a medium flame and keep stirring till the onion becomes soft and pink. Add the marinated mutton and fry non-stop for 7 minutes till red-brown. Add the ground masala, lower the heat and cook for 10 minutes stirring all the time. Add 2 litres of water and cover with a tight-fitting lid. Add water on top of the lid and cook over a low to medium flame for 2½ hours till the mutton is tender. Taste for salt. Keep checking on the meat every 20 minutes or so. Keep topping up the water on the lid. When necessary, add more water to the mutton and stir.

• Do not cook the rice till soft. Add a little less water than usual. After the rice is ready, wait for the mutton to become tender. Gently stir the rice

FOR THE GROUND MASALA

6	green chillies deseeded	
1	tbsp. black peppercorns	
6	green cardamoms seeds only	
8	cloves	Grind
1″	piece cinnamon	in a
2	tbsps. red chilli powder	quarter
2	tbsps. turmeric powder	cup of
2	tbsps. coriander seeds	water
1	tbsp. cumin seeds	
1	tbsp. poppy seeds	
½	tbsp. shahjeera	
½	tbsp. dry ginger powder	

FOR THE DECORATION

2   sliced onions deep fried till crisp

and place it on top of the cooked mutton. Cover with a tight lid and seal the vessel with dough. Place the vessel on a large iron tava over medium heat for 45 minutes. Allow to settle for 5 minutes.

- Open the vessel and serve the rice and meat on a flat dish covered with the fried onions.

Accompaniments:

Vegetable dish of frenchbeans and coconut

Cold cucumber raita

Hot lime pickle

Stewed cold Apples as dessert

JEHANGIRI PULAO TAZE FALON KE SAATH

- Preparation Time: 30 mins. • Marinating Time: 1½ hours • Cooking Time: 50 mins.
- Serves: 6-8

FOR THE RICE

1	gm. saffron
850	gms. basmati rice
200	gms. dried apricots washed
200	gms. golden raisins washed
50	gms. dried figs
4	bay leaves
1	tsp. carraway seeds broiled

Salt, Ghee

FOR THE FRESH FRUITS

6	peaches skinned and cubed
6	apples skinned cubed and sprinkled with lime juice
1	fresh ripe pineapple skinned and cubed
4	red plums skinned and cubed
4	orange plums skinned and cubed
2	sweet limes skinned and sectioned
3	oranges squeezed for juice
2	tbsps. castor sugar

FOR THE MUTTON

1200	gms. boneless mutton, cubed preferably – from the leg portion
500	gms. cream or clotted cream
2	litres rich milk
10	whole peppercorns
4	cardamoms seeds only
1½	tbsps. fresh ginger pounded

Salt, Ghee

FOR THE DECORATION

½	cup almonds boiled sliced fried
½	cup pistachios boiled sliced fried
½	cup whole large salted cashewnuts
¼	cup pine nuts fried
¼	cup cucumber nuts fried
¼	cup watermelon seeds
4	sheets of silver vark or foil

- Marinate the meat in salt and pounded ginger for ½ an hour, after which marinate in the milk for atleast an hour.

- Meanwhile wash the dried fruits and cook them in the rice cooker along with the rice, bay leaves, carraway seeds, salt and ghee. Use a little less ghee. Do not allow the rice to become soft.

- Place the meat, spices and milk in a pressure cooker and cook till soft. If there is some milky soup left, do not dry it. Heat the saffron on a griddle and crumble into the cooked meat gravy. Simmer over a low fire for 10 minutes.

- Place the meat and its gravy into a large pan. Whisk the cream and spread it over the meat. Sprinkle lightly with a little fine salt. Then place the rice over the meat and close the vessel with a lid and seal with dough. Place over a large iron tava over a medium flame for 20 minutes.

- Remove the hot rice and meat on a silver salver and cover with the fresh fruits sprinkled with sugar. Place less than ⅓ of the fruit on top of the pulao. Place the rest around it. Top the rice with fried nuts and silver foil.

- If you like you can substitute the fresh fruits with canned peaches, pineapples, apricots, cherries and pears.

Accompaniments:

Apricot chutney

White chicken curry

Lashings of sweet curd topped with saffron water

Fresh strawberry Ice-cream

HYDERABADI PAYA KA PULAO

- Preparation Time: 30 mins. • Cooking Time: 2 hours in a pressure cooker or 6 hours on a charcoal sigri • Serves: 15-20

FOR THE TROTTERS

25	front leg trotters each cut into 3 pieces
4	tbsps. ginger-garlic paste
1	tbsp. black pepper powder
Salt	

FOR THE MASALA

2	tbsps. coriander seeds broiled
2	tbsps. cumin seeds broiled
2	tbsps. fennel seeds broiled
1	large pod garlic
2"	stick cinnamon
6	cloves
15	black peppercorns
1	whole bunch fresh coriander, chopped fine
12	green chillies deseeded
½	fresh coconut grated
	milk of 1 fresh coconut
6	whole onions chopped, deep fried and pounded
2	tsps. dried ginger powder
Juice of 2 sour limes	
Salt	

Grind in water

FOR THE RICE

1200 gms. basmati rice
4 bay leaves
Salt
Ghee

- Grind the masala very fine and set aside.

- Wash the trotters 3 times. Each one should be cut into 3 pieces. So altogether you should have 75 pieces. Marinate the trotters in salt and the ginger-garlic paste.

- If you wish you can put the trotters with 4 litres of water in a large vessel which you can place on a coal sigri early in the morning and allow to cook over a slow fire for 6 hours. You must cover with a tight fitting lid and seal with dough.

OR

You can cook in a large pressure cooker or 2 medium sized cookers for atleast 2 hours after the whistle goes, on a very low fire.

- After you open the pressure cooker or large vessel allow the soup to evaporate over a medium-high flame so that finally you are left with the bones and a thick jelly-like soup. Taste for salt.

- Take a large vessel and place the pounded fried onion in it along with 3 tablespoons of ghee. Place on a medium fire and when it heats up add the finely ground masala. Lower the heat and cook the masala for 7 minutes till well mixed and fried. Then add the coconut milk and allow to simmer for 5 minutes. Put in the cooked trotters and the thick soup and stir for 5 minutes. Allow to simmer for 10 more minutes.

- Wash the rice 3 times. Then mix in fine salt, bay leaves and some ghee — about 2 tablespoons or so. Place the rice on top of the trotters and soup and close the lid tightly with dough. Place on an iron tava over medium heat for 1½ hours.

- Please check that the liquid you have will be enough to cook your rice. Actually, you should have enough soup left to cook the rice. If you have evaporated too much of it, make it up with the coconut milk or water.

Accompaniments:
Minced meat
Dahiwadas
Elaichi and mango chutney
Falooda or Kulfi

PUKKE AAM KA GOSHT PULAO

FOR THE RICE

850 gms. basmati rice
4 bay leaves
½ cup pink rose petals
2 onions sliced and deep fried
Salt
Ghee

FOR THE MANGOES

8 ripe mangoes peeled cut into
  cubes
1 cup sugar
2 cups water
2 gms. saffron

FOR THE MUTTON

1200 gms. boneless mutton
500 gms. cream or clotted cream
3 onions sliced, fried and pounded
  into a pulp
2 tbsps. garam masala
4 green cardamoms bruised
1 tsp. each powdered sesame seeds,
  carraway seeds, poppy seeds
4 mace flowers
2 tbsps. fresh ginger pulped
Salt
Ghee

- Cook the rice with bay leaves, salt and ghee.
- Marinate the meat in the ginger pulp and salt for ½ an hour.
- Place the pulped fried onion in a vessel along with 2 tablespoons of ghee. When it gets hot, add the meat and fry till red. Lower the flame and add the garam masala, mace, cardamoms and stir-fry for 5 minutes, after which you sprinkle the carraway, poppy and sesame powders. Stir non-stop for another 5 minutes and transfer the mutton to pressure cooker. Add water and cook till tender.
- Place the sugar and water in a flat bottomed pan. Add heated crumbled saffron and bring the syrup to a boil. When the syrup starts bubbling, add the mango pieces and shake the vessel with both your hands, holding it tight with kitchen towels. Allow to simmer for 5 minutes and cool.
- Spread the rice on a thali. Mix in the rose petals, and fried sliced onions.
- Place the cooked mutton in a large dekchi, after greasing it well. Whip the cream lightly and spread over the mutton. Cover with the rice. Take the mango pieces and arrange over the rice. Cover the vessel with a lid and seal with dough. Place it on an iron tava for 15 minutes over a medium flame.
- Serve the pulao on a silver dish taking care to take it out with the help of a porcelain quarter plate. Heap it so that everyone gets the mutton and the mangoes.

Accompaniments:

Chicken Liver Sauté
A salad of cooked vegetables
Brinjal pickle
Malai sandwiches with lichi ice-cream

NOOR JEHAN KA BEMISAL PULAO

• Preparation Time: 30 mins. • Marinating Time: 1 hour • Cooking Time: 1 hour • Serves: 8-10

FOR THE RICE

300	gms. basmati rice
1	cup pink rose petals
½	tsp. rose essence
6	drops pink colour
2	tbsps. sugar

Salt
Ghee

1	gm. saffron
200	gms. basmati rice
3	onions sliced and fried
4	cloves
4	green cardamoms bruised
2"	stick cinnamon

Salt
Ghee

300	gms. basmati rice
1	tsp. crushed carraway seeds
½	tsp. mace powder
8	black peppercorns
4	bay leaves
4 – 6	drops green food colouring

Salt
Ghee

The pulao is assembled with three types of coloured rice, mutton chunks with gravy, boneless chicken with gravy, kababs, fried potatoes, fried paneer with a formidable topping of nuts and cherries.

FOR THE MUTTON

500	gms. meat chunks with nali
400	gms. yogurt
2	large onions chopped
1	tbsp. ginger garlic paste
2	tbsps. garam masala
3	green cardamoms crushed
1	tsp. carraway seeds crushed
7	black peppercorns crushed

Salt
Ghee

• Prepare all three types of rice separately and then cool and place them separately in a large thali. Mix the boiled grated beetroot lightly with one-third of the rice and set apart. One-third rice will be saffron and another light green.

• Marinate the meat in the salt, ginger-garlic paste, garam masala and the yogurt and keep aside for 1 hour. Heat 2 tablespoons of ghee and when hot, add the cardamoms, carraway seeds and peppercorns, fry for 2 minutes, lower flame and add the chopped onions and cook till pink and soft. Then add the mutton and yogurt and cook in a pressure cooker till soft.

• Place the chopped onions for the chicken and 2 tablespoons of ghee and cook till the onion is soft and pink. Salt the chicken and cook it with the onions for 7 minutes after which lower the flame and add the ginger powder, shahjeera, coriander seeds, cumin and fennel powder. Cook for 3 minutes stirring all the time and then add the pulped tomatoes. Reduce the heat to low, cover and place water on the lid and cook till soft. Keep pouring the hot water from the lid into the chicken till it is soft and you have a thick gravy. Remove the chicken from the stove, whip or mix the cream lightly and add it to the chicken. Stir well. Taste.

• Except for the oil, mix all the items for the kababs together. Mix well, form into small, even-sized balls. Heat oil in a karhai. Wet your hands, roll the balls and place in hot oil till golden brown. Roll them in the silver vark or silver foil. Set aside.

• Take a little pure ghee (½ a cup) and lightly sauté the paneer in it. Set aside.

FOR THE CHICKEN

600 gms. boneless chicken
200 gms. cream
2 large onions finely chopped
200 gms. pulped tomatoes
1½ tsps. ginger powder
1 tbsp. crushed shahjeera
1 tbsp. coriander seeds broiled powdered
1 tsp. fennel powdered
½ tsp. cumin broiled and crushed
Salt
Ghee

FOR THE KABABS

200 gms. mutton mince
150 gms. potatoes mashed
1 tsp. black pepper powder
1 tsp. coriander powder
½ tsp. cardamom powder
½ tsp. mace
1 tbsp. ginger crushed
2 tbsps. fresh coriander ground
2 eggs
Juice of one sour lime
Silver vark
Salt
Peanut oil

FOR THE EXTRAS

300 gms. creamy paneer cut into flat rectangular pieces
150 gms. potatoes peeled, cubed, fried
1 beetroot boiled grated
4 sheets silver vark or foil

FOR THE TOPPING

1 cup sliced fried almonds
½ cup sliced fried pistachios
¼ cup musk melon seeds
¼ cup cucumber seeds
¼ cup watermelon seeds
¼ cup pumpkin seeds
½ can cherries

• Take a large biryani vessel. Grease the base and sides well. Divide the rice into 3 portions. Place a large layer of rice at the bottom, sprinkle some beetroot rice on top of it and then layer it with the cooked meat and fried potatoes. Sprinkle half the silver covered meatballs on top along with half the paneer. Place a layer of saffron rice on top of the meat sprinkle with some· of the beetroot rice and arrange the boneless chicken on it. Cover with the remaining meatballs, paneer and fried potatoes. Then place the remaining green rice on top of it, sprinkle the beetroot rice and then top it with circles of cherries. Scatter the assorted fried nuts over the cherries and seal the lid with dough. Place on an iron tava over a medium flame for 25 minutes.

• This great pulao needs no accompaniment as such. You can serve sweet mango chutney with it. Genuine Moghul recipes did not contain chillies.

Optional Accompaniments:

Stir-fried ladyfingers with fresh grated coconut

Salad of fresh cut vegetables and fruits

Sweet curd with chopped ripe mangoes or stoned cherries or cut peaches

Almond – Pista – Raisin Ice-cream

DUMBO MURGHI PULAO BHARELO
(A Whole Roasted Lamb or Kid Stuffed with Chicken Pulao)

• Preparation Time: 1½ hours • Marinating Time: 5-10 hours • Cooking Time: almost 6 hours
• Serves: 50

FOR THE KID OR LAMB

8-10	kgs.	tender lamb or kid without the head
5	gms.	saffron
4-5	tbsps.	ginger-garlic paste
3	kgs.	curd or yogurt
3	tbsps.	tenderizer
5	kgs.	ghee
Salt		

GROUND MASALA FOR THE KID OR LAMB

30	red kashmiri chillies deseeded	
40	black peppercorns	Grind in
4"	stick cinnamon	half a cup of
10	cloves	sugarcane
4	pods of garlic	vinegar
200	gms. cleaned tamarind	
Salt		

FOR THE CHICKEN PULAO

2	gms.	saffron
1	kg.	basmati rice
2½	kgs.	chicken breast each cut into 3-4 pieces
4		onions finely chopped
4		onions sliced and deep fried
300	gms.	red tomatoes skinned and chopped
12		boiled eggs whole
300	gms.	seedless raisins
300	gms.	salted cashewnuts
150	gms.	dried apricots soaked overnight
Salt		
Ghee		

• Wash the kid well inside and out till it is completely clean. Then marinate it in salt and the ginger-garlic paste. Poke it all over with a small thin iron rod. Whisk the curd along with the tenderizer and smear it all over the kid's body inside and out.

• Grind the masala very fine and smear it all over the kid and marinate it for 5-10 hours.

• The next morning make the chicken pulao. Wash the chicken breasts and cut each into 3-4 pieces and marinate in salt, ginger, garlic and the chicken pulao ground masala. Cook the chopped onions in ½ a cup of ghee and when soft add the marinated chicken. Lower the heat, and stir the chicken, cover and cook in its own juice for 10 minutes. When the chicken has fried well, add the tomatoes and 2 cups of water and cook on the same low heat till tender and allow most of the moisture to dry up.

• Divide the rice into 2 portions. Cook ½ with the saffron and cook the other plain white, in a rice cooker. Take a large thala and mix the two rice. Then take a vessel and mix up the rice and the chicken, the fried onion, raisins, cashewnuts and apricots.

1. *Grilled Chicken Drumsticks Pulao*
2. *Tandoori Chicken Thigh Pulao smothered in cream and curd.*

GROUND MASALA FOR THE CHICKEN PULAO

1½"	stick cinnamon	
10	peppercorns	
2	star anise	Dry grind
6	cloves	
1	tsp. shahjeera	
4	mace flowers	

- Stuff the chicken pulao along with the boiled eggs into the kid's stomach. Sew up the stomach and neck cavities with a large iron needle and thick white cord.

- Take a huge flat-bottomed vessel. If you don't possess one borrow or hire it. Wash it well twice and dry it. Make a coal fire in a large sigri and place the vessel upon it. Add 3 kilos of ghee, allow to melt and then 2 people should pick up the kid and place it carefully in the hot ghee. Be careful that your hands don't get singed. Then with the help of a ladle pour hot ghee from the sides of the vessel onto the kid. Turn the kid over and allow to fry on the other side and cook till red. Keep hot water ready and pour 2 litres at a time to cook the mutton. Keep over medium heat for as many hours as it takes to cook the meat till soft and tender.

- When you feel that the meat is almost ready, broil 5 gms. of saffron on an iron tava over a low heat and sprinkle on the meat till the aroma of the cooking saffron fills the air. Cover the meat and keep it warm till the meal starts.

- Serve on a large silver platter or a tray surrounded by lettuce, cucumbers, tomato slices and cut sweet limes, oranges and bunches of green and black grapes.

Accompaniments:

Masala chicken livers

Fried chicken farchas

Apple and tomato hot sauce with whole garlic cloves

Boondi Raita

Mango Ice-cream

1. *Khade Murgyon ka Aflatoon Pulao*
2. *Jalebis*

SHIRAZI PULAO

• Preparation Time: 30 mins. • Cooking Time: 1 hour • Serves: 6-8

FOR THE RICE

1	gm. saffron
1	pinch saffron colour
600	gms. basmati rice
4	bay leaves
2"	piece cinnamon
3	star anise
2	onions sliced and deep fried
½	cup pure ghee
Salt	

FOR THE MUTTON

2	gms. saffron
750	gms. mutton pieces with nali
3	large onions chopped
6	large tomatoes skinned and chopped
Salt, Ghee	

FOR THE GROUND MASALA

5	mace flowers
1"	cinnamon
4	cloves
2"	piece dried coconut
15	black peppercorns
1	tsp. shahjeera

Grind fine with ¼ cup of water

FOR THE KABABS

250	gms. minced mutton
1	onion finely minced
½	tbsp. ginger-garlic paste
8	slices stale bread
1½	tbsps. fresh curd
½	cup fresh coriander chopped
2	tbsps. fresh mint chopped
4	green chillies deseeded and chopped fine (optional)
1	tsp. fennel powder
½	tsp. star anise powder
3	eggs
Salt, Refined oil	

• Divide the rice into 2 portions. Cook one portion with the spices and sliced fried onions and one portion with the saffron and saffron colour in a rice cooker. Separate the grains with a fork and spread out on a thali.

• Wash the mutton well and marinate in the salt and ginger-garlic paste. Then place the chopped onions in a vessel and add ½ a cup of ghee to it. Place on medium heat and allow to cook till soft. Add the ground masala and stir well for 5 minutes on a low heat. Add the tomatoes, cook for a further 5 minutes and then add the mutton. Place it in a pressure cooker with sufficient water so that the mutton is cooked soft, and one cup of gravy remains.

• Place the mince in a thali and mix it with the salt and ginger-garlic paste. Add the finely chopped coriander, mint and the green chillies, if using them. Soak the bread in water, squeeze the water out, shred it finely and mix in the yogurt and add to the mince. Mix well. Beat the eggs into the mince mixture vigorously and form into tiny balls. You should get 20-28 small kababs. Wet your palms, form the kababs, and deep fry in hot oil till golden brown.

• Place the cooked white rice in a large vessel. Cover it with the cooked meat and gravy and top it with the fried meat balls. Then cover with the yellow — saffron rice. Cover with a lid and seal with dough. Place on an iron tava over medium heat for ½ an hour.

• Remove the pulao onto a round or oval dish, cover with the fried onions, fried almonds, soaked apricots and raisins.

FOR THE DECORATION

20	dried apricots soaked overnight in sugar water
½	cup seedless raisins soaked overnight in sugar, white vinegar and water
½	cup whole almonds blanched, skinned and deep-fried
6	boiled eggs cut into halves
3	onions sliced and deep-fried a crisp golden brown

Accompaniments:

Hot green chilli pickle

Lettuce and cucumber salad smothered in sugar and lemon dressing

A thick mutton gravy

Potato salan

Rose ice-cream

BADSHAHI KESRI PULAO

- Preparation Time: 20 mins. • Marinating Time: 2 hours • Cooking Time: 1 hour 25 mins.
  • Serves: 8-10

FOR THE RICE

2	gms. saffron
650	gms. basmati rice
2	onions sliced and deep fried
4	large brown cardamoms
4	allspice corns or leaves
8	black peppercorns
1	tbsp. Ghee
Salt	

FOR THE MUTTON

1250	gms. mutton pieces along with nali
1½	tbsps. ginger-garlic paste
300	gms. thick curd or yogurt
3	large onions chopped fine
2	large onions sliced and deep fried
4	large potatoes skinned, cubed and deep fried
5	large tomatoes skinned and chopped
Salt, Ghee	

FOR THE GROUND MASALA

8	kashmiri chillies	
1"	piece cinnamon	
14	black peppercorns	
4	cloves	Grind
4	green cardamom seeds crushed	in a ¼ cup of water
1	tsp. fennel seeds	
½	tsp. carraway seeds	
½	cup fresh coriander	
1"	ambahalad	

FOR THE DECORATION

2	onions deep fried
½	cup raisins deep fried
½	cup whole cashewnuts deep fried
100	gms. pistachios boiled, sliced and fried
4	sheets of silver vark
Half a cup pink rose petals	

- Cook the rice with all its ingredients in a rice cooker.

- Wash the mutton well and marinate in salt and ginger-garlic paste. Set aside in a cool place.

- Grind the masala on a grinding stone or mixie. Reserve the water with which you have washed the stone or the mixie. Mix the masala into the curd and whip it well. Apply it to the mutton and set aside for 2 hours.

- When the 2 hours are up, place the chopped onions in a vessel with one cup of pure ghee and put on medium flame. Cook till soft and then add the marinated mutton and allow to sizzle. Stir for 7 to 10 minutes. Add 3 cups of water and pressure cook till soft.

- Place half the rice in a large vessel. Cover with the cooked meat and the fried potatoes. Then cover with the remaining rice mixed with rose petals. Close with a well fitting lid, seal with dough and place over an iron tava for ½ hour.

- Remove the rice on a silver platter and cover lavishly with the fried onions, raisins, cashewnuts, fried pistachios and 4 sheets of silver vark.

Accompaniments:

Sweet tomato and apple chutney

Cold beetroot salad

A dish of boneless chicken

Chikoo ice-cream

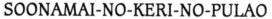

SOONAMAI-NO-KERI-NO-PULAO
(An old Parsi favourite from the villages of Gujarat)

• Preparation Time: 20 mins. • Cooking Time: 2½ hours • Serves: 6-8

There was a tree near the huge gate in my great grandmother Soonamai's yard which yielded large saffron flushed mangoes which were very sweet. Delicious meals were prepared with these mangoes on special days. This pulao was one of them.

FOR THE RICE
600 gms. long grained rice
2 onions sliced and fried
10 black peppercorns
1" cinnamon
3 bay leaves
Salt, Ghee

FOR THE MANGOES
6 alphonso or any other large mangoes
½ tsp. nutmeg-cardamom powder
2 tbsps. fine sugar

FOR THE MUTTON
1¼ kg. mutton chunks
1½ tbsps. ginger-garlic paste
3 large onions chopped
2 tbsps. garam masala
6 whole red dried chillies
3 mace flowers
1 tsp. shahjeera
Salt, Ghee

FOR THE DECORATION
Some sheets of silver vark or sliced almonds

• Cook the rice along with the fried onions, black peppercorns, cinnamon, bay leaves, salt and 1 tablespoon of ghee in a rice cooker, after the mutton has been cooked.

• Wash the mutton and marinate it in salt and the ginger-garlic paste.

• Place the chopped onions along with 1 cup of ghee in a large vessel and cook till soft. Then add the dried chillies, mace flowers and shahjeera. Stir for 1 minute and add the mutton. Stir vigorously and fry till red. Add the garam masala and fry for 2 more minutes. Add 2 to 3 cups of water. Cover with a lid and put water on it. Lower the flame and allow to cook till soft and tender. Keep checking every 15 minutes or so that the water does not dry up and keep replacing with hot water in the vessel and on the lid.

• Peel the mangoes and cut pieces from the cheeks and sides. Place them in a small saucepan and sprinkle sugar. Add ½ a cup of water and allow it to come to a boil. Cool.

• When the meat has been cooked to total tenderness, set out the hot rice on a platter and cover with the meat. Top it with the mangoes sprinkled with the nutmeg-cardamom powder. Cover with the silver sheets or sliced almonds.

Accompaniments:
A garlic sweet and sour pickle
Onion tomato kachumber
Fried prawns and pomfret slices
A cold dish of vermicelli cooked in milk and pistachios

THE SHALIMAR FRAGRANT PULAO
(The Pulao of Pulaos)

• Preparation Time: 30 mins. • Marinating Time: 2 hours • Cooking Time: 1½ hours
• Serves: 10-12

This is a very unusual pulao. It consists of 6 different colours and 6 different fragrances.

FOR THE RICE
900 gms basmati rice divided into Six parts and cooked in a rice cooker

1] WHITE RICE
Cook with 2 tbsp. boiled, skinned, ground almond paste, 4 cloves whole, salt and ghee. Top the rice with fresh or canned chopped ripe mangoes.

2] PINK RICE
Cook with a few (4-6) drops of cochineal colour, 1 tablespoon of sugar, ½ teaspoon of rose essence, salt and ghee. Top with pink rose petals.

3] GREEN RICE
Cook with (4-6) drops of green food colour, 4 heavily pounded cardamoms, salt and ghee. Top with fried almond slivers.

4] LEMON RICE
Cook with the juice of 2 sour limes, a pinch of lemon pulao colouring, salt and ghee. Top with boiled green peas and fresh lime slices.

5] TOMATO RICE
Cook with a pinch of tomato pulao colour, 2 cups of tomato juice, ½ teaspoon oregano, salt and ghee. Top it with diamond shapes cut from red and golden peppers.

6] SAFFRON RICE
Cook with 1 gm. saffron, salt and ghee and 2 cups of Pineapple juice. Top with canned chopped pineapple pieces.

FOR THE MUTTON
1	kg. mutton chunks with nali
500	gms. boneless mutton chunks
25	gms. ginger crushed ground
20	gms. garlic crushed
500	gms. thick curd or yogurt
2″	cinnamon
6	cloves
20	black peppercorns
10	kashmiri chillies
1	tsp. shahjeera
1	tsp. carraway seeds
4	mace flowers
4	star anise

Broil lightly on a tava and dry grind in a mixie

• Wash the mutton, salt and marinate it in the crushed ginger, garlic and yogurt for 2 hours.

• Cook the onions in 1½ cups of ghee till golden brown. Add the broiled spice masala and stir for 3 minutes. Then add the mutton chunks along with all the marinate and cook over a low heat, covered, till tender. This will take atleast 2½ hours. In a pressure cooker it will be tender in 35 minutes. Use the method you prefer.

• Lay out the table with your best silver vessels. Have a beautiful cloth piece or a painting as your background.

500	gms. onions finely chopped
250	gms. onions sliced and deep fried
4	potatoes peeled, cut into large cubes and fried

Salt, Ghee

TO SERVE

* Keep a salver ready and place the 6 different kinds of rice in an oval design around the rim. In the centre of the dish, arrange the cooked mutton and nali chunks and top with the fried potato cubes and fried onions.

* The pulao may be served with a dish of mutton chops, Sali-marghi, lettuce mixed with strawberries, boiled gourd raita and toffee ice-cream.

Accompaniments:

Almonds, pistas and raisins in a chutney sauce

A green salad with avocados, lettuce, celery and apples

A green chilli and banana raita

Fresh fruits and chikoo ice-cream

A PULAO OF LIVER AND PEACHES IN CREAM

• Preparation Time: 20 mins. • Cooking Time: 1 hour 45 mins. • Serves: 6-8

FOR THE RICE

400	gms. basmati rice
2	tsps. oil
Salt	

FOR THE LIVER

4	onions sliced deep fried
6	large sweet green chillies
1	large goat's liver, washed, skinned and chopped into small pieces
1"	fresh ginger cut julienne
1"	fresh ambahalad cut julienne
1	tsp. turmeric powder
1	tsp. chilli powder
½	tsp. ground cinnamon powder
½	tsp. ground clove powder
½	tsp. ground black peppercorn powder
½	tsp. ground cardamom powder
½	tsp. ground mace powder
½	tsp. ground fennel powder
½	tsp. ground mustard powder
Salt	
Sunflower oil	

FOR THE PEACHES

4	litres milk boiled 4 times the day before and chilled in the refrigerator for its clotted cream
8	large fresh peaches skinned, halved and stoned
16	half pieces walnuts
½	cup sugar
A few spring onions, cut julienne	

• First cook the rice in an electric rice cooker with salt and 2 teaspoons of oil. Remove onto a tray, cool and separate the rice grains.

• Grind the fried onions and place in a wok or karhai over a very low heat. Add the green chillies, ginger, ambahalad and cook gently for 3 minutes. Mix the liver with salt, turmeric, chilli and the spice powders and add to the onions. Raise the fire a wee bit, add ½ cup water and mix well and simmer for 12 minutes till the tiny pieces of liver are well cooked.

• Take the rice and gradually mix into the wok until it is well amalgamated with the liver. Keep hot.

• Place ½ a cup of sugar and 1 cup of water in a flat vessel. Allow the sugar to melt and carefully place the peach halves in the syrup and poach the peaches for 10 minutes on a low flame. Spoon the syrup onto the peach halves.

• Arrange the hot rice in the centre of a flat dish and surround it with the hot peach halves. Pour a little of the clotted cream into each peach hollow and top each with half a walnut piece.

• Sprinkle as much of the spring onions, as desirable to you and serve immediately.

Accompaniments:

Jellied Russian Salad

Boneless Chicken Gravy

Sweet fruit chutney

Vanilla ice-cream with almond macaroons

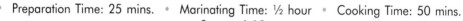

KERALA CHICKEN BIRYANI

- Preparation Time: 25 mins. • Marinating Time: ½ hour • Cooking Time: 50 mins.
- Serves: 6-10

FOR THE RICE

800	gms. basmati rice
2	potatoes skinned and cubed
2	onions sliced and fried crisp
3	green cardamoms crushed
4	bay leaves

Salt, Ghee

FOR THE CHICKEN

3	free range chickens cut into small pieces OR
1600	gms. broiler chicken cut into small pieces
2	tbsps. ginger garlic paste ⎫
12	black peppercorns crushed ⎬ Whole spices
4	green cardamoms crushed ⎭
4	cloves
4	½" sticks cinnamon
3-5	sprigs curry leaves
4	onions finely chopped
500	gms. large red tomatoes skinned
400	gms. curd
6	slit green chillies

Juice of 1 sour lime
Salt, Ghee

FOR THE GROUND MASALA

½	coconut grated and milk removed	⎫
150	gms. cashew nuts	⎪ Grind
2	tbsps. broiled coriander seeds	⎬ in a little
1	tsp. cumin	⎪ water
6-8	red reshampatti chillies	⎪
1"	piece of turmeric	⎭

FOR THE DECORATION

Very finely sliced coconut chips ½ cup
Very finely sliced potato slices 2 cups
100 gms. fried raisins

- Cook the rice with all its ingredients in a rice cooker.

- Wash the chicken well twice. Marinate in salt, ginger-garlic paste and the sour lime juice for half an hour.

- Chop the onions finely and place in a large vessel with the whole spices, 1¼ cups ghee, curry sprigs and cook over a medium fire till soft and pink. Add the marinated chicken and the slit green chillies and allow to fry in its own juice for 5 minutes. Stir and lower the heat and cook for another 5 minutes. Add the ground masala and stir well and allow to fry a little for 5 minutes. Add the finely chopped skinned tomatoes and cover tightly with a lid and cook over a very low flame. Place water on the lid. Keep checking on the chicken so it does not burn and keep adding the hot water from the lid. When the chicken is soft and tender there should be a cup of gravy in the vessel. Whisk the curd into the chicken and cook for 5 more minutes.

- Take the cooked rice and place it over the chicken. Sprinkle ½ cup of warm water over the rice cover tightly with a lid and dough. Place over coals or on a hot iron tava over gas on a medium flame for ½ an hour.

- Remove onto a large dish and decorate with the crisply fried thin coconut slices, potato slices and raisins.

Accompaniments:

Mixed Vegetable Raita
Cucumber-Tomato Salad
Coconut Payasam

KHADE MURGYON KA AFLATOON PULAO

- Preparation Time: 25-30 mins • Cooking Time + Stitching time: 1 hour-1 hour 15 mins.
- Serves: 6

Many Parsi gentlemen worked for the Nizam of Hyderabad and his innumerable Nawabs and the Royal Princes. Those who spent their sweat and blood for the Nizam and dealt with scrupulous honesty where his treasures were concerned were given the title of Khan-Saheb. This title was worn with pride and gratitude. These men brought back to their families in Gujarat, some of the sophistication of the Hyderabadi court. Their ladies were heavily decked out in pearls, emeralds and jewellery and their kitchens also underwent a subtle change. They cooked with cream, yogurt, sugar and spices and this included the use of entire spring chickens fried, stuffed and used in pulaos. Meat was drenched in home made pure ghee and a fashion was started wherein the old Persian rites of using rose petals, saffron and dried fruits were revived. The last time I was served an entire chicken was 30 years ago at the wedding of Dasturji Jamasp-Asa of Bombay. It is now a dying art to create pulaos from these stuffed whole baby chickens.

FOR THE RICE

1	gm. saffron
450	gms. basmati rice
150	gms. potatoes peeled cubed
3	onions sliced and deep fried
3	cloves
3	crushed green cardamoms
1	tsp. shahjeera
Salt	
Ghee	

FOR THE CHICKEN

6	whole spring chickens
1	tbsp. ginger garlic paste
Salt	
Ghee preferably pure ghee	
Peanut oil	

FOR THE STUFFING

1	thick large needle and white cord
6	boiled eggs
700	gms. mutton mince
1	large onion finely chopped
2	tbsps. coriander freshly chopped
1	tbsp. mint freshly chopped
1	tsp. garam masala

- Cook the rice in a rice cooker along with the saffron, potatoes, onions, cloves, cardamoms, shahjeera, salt and ghee.

- Wash the whole chickens inside and out thoroughly 3 times. Leave 1" of the neck intact. Marinate in salt and ginger-garlic paste and set aside in a cool place.

- Prepare the stuffing by frying the onion in 1 tablespoon of ghee. After it turns golden brown, add the mince and salt and cook over a low fire, in its own juice. After 5 minutes add the salt, spices, ground chillies, mint and coriander and cook stirring the mince all the time. Add one cup of water and cook the mince till tender. If the mince is still tough add some more water and allow the mince to dry. Taste for salt.

- Stuff each chicken with one boiled egg and mince and stitch it from both sides. Then half fill a very large karhai with oil and place on high heat. When the oil heats up, lower the flame and deep fry each chicken one at a time till golden brown. Place the chickens in a large vessel, add

1   tsp. Parsi dhansakh masala
3   red chillies ground in a little water
½   tsps. anise crushed and carraway
        seeds
Salt
Ghee

FOR THE DECORATION

4   sheets of silver foil
50   gms. fried raisins
Rose petals from 3 roses

3 cups hot water, cover and cook till tender. Add more water if the chicken is not tender and very soft. Taste the remaining gravy for salt. Tip the cooked rice over the chickens. Sprinkle 1 cup of water over the rice and seal the vessel with a lid and dough. Place on a large tava and cook on a charcoal fire for half an hour.

- Remove on a platter and decorate with fried raisins, rose petals and silver foil.

Accompaniments:

Parsi Dhansakh Dal

Salad of Spring Onions, Cucumber, Carrots, Beetroots and Apples

Boondi Raita

Malai Kulfi

KESAR KALIA AUR ZAFFRANI PULAO

- Preparation Time: 25 mins.   •   Cooking Time: 45 mins.   •   Serves: 6-8

Kalia is a mutton or chicken dish cooked in Northern India. At the royal palaces Kalias were cooked with saffron, almonds, pistachios, mawa, milk, curd, pure ghee and expensive spices. In this recipe I have tried to combine two recipes in one. I hope you like the combination.

FOR THE RICE

2   gms. saffron
700   gms. basmati rice
150   gms. mawa
2   large onions sliced
4   bay leaves
4   green cardamom seeds bruised
1   tbsp. coriander seeds broiled
        and coarsely ground
1   litre milk
2   tbsps. ghee
Salt

- Place the sliced onions and ghee in a large vessel. Fry till soft and pink. Add the bay leaves, cardamom seeds, coriander seeds and the washed rice. Cook for 5 minutes and transfer the rice into a rice cooker. Add the heated saffron and one litre of milk and the extra water needed to cook the rice. Mash the mawa with your fingers and loosen it. Beat lightly with a fork and add it to the rice. Add salt and cook till the rice is tender. Spread out on a thali to cool.

MASALA FOR THE CHICKEN

25	almonds boiled and skinned	
20	cashew nuts	
10	red kashmiri chillies	
1	tbsp. poppy seeds	
1	tbsp. coriander seeds broiled	Grind very fine in one cup water
1	tbsp. fennel seeds broiled	
1"	piece cinnamon	
3	green cardamoms seeds only	
2	cloves	
5	allspice berries	

FOR THE KALIA

1200 gms. boneless chicken cut into 1½" pieces.
1   tbsp. ginger garlic paste
1   tsp. black pepper powder
1   tsp. mace
½   fresh coconut grated for its milk
2   onions finely chopped
2-3   tbsps. ghee or more
Salt

FOR THE DECORATION

2   onions sliced fried
4   boiled eggs
2   tbsps. pistachios boiled sliced fried
100   gms. raisins washed and fried

- Take a large vessel and put 3 tablespoons of ghee in it. Place on medium heat. Marinate the chicken in salt, pepper and the ginger-garlic paste and place into the vessel in hot ghee. Fry the pieces till red and remove from the pan. Add the onions and cook over medium heat till soft. Add the ground masala and roast for 10 minutes. Add the coconut milk and mace and allow the gravy to boil. When it has boiled add the fried chicken pieces and lower the flame to the lowest point and cover and cook till the chicken softens.

- Take a vessel and grease its sides and bottom and place half the rice in it. Then place the chicken Kalia on top of the rice and cover it with the remaining rice. Sprinkle a quarter cup of water on top of the rice.

- Decorate with halved or quartered boiled eggs, sliced onions, fried raisins and pistachios. Cover with foil or a lid and dough. Place on an iron griddle over a medium flame for 15 minutes on dum. Place a few live coals on top of the cover.

- Open at the table so you can savour the aroma.

Accompaniments:

Sweet Curd

Chicken livers in masala

Gulabjamuns and pistachios

SAFED MURGH KA PULAO

• Preparation Time: 25 mins. • Cooking Time: 55 mins. • Serves: 8-10

FOR THE RICE

2	gms. saffron
450	gms. basmati rice
1	tsp. carraway seeds
1	tsp. coriander seeds broiled crushed
3/4	litre milk
Salt	
Pure ghee	

FOR THE CHICKEN

1	litre milk
1	kg. boneless chicken pieces 1½" in size
4	medium onions finely chopped
1½	tbsps. ginger-garlic paste
½	cup pink rose petals
Milk of 1 large coconut	
Salt	

FOR THE MASALA

1	tbsp. sesame seeds
1	tbsp. coriander seeds
1	tbsp. fennel seeds
10	deseeded green chillies
1	large pod garlic
1	tea cup cashewnuts broken
1	tea cup almonds boiled skinned

} Grind with one cup water

FOR THE DECORATION

3	sheets silver vark

• Cook the rice in milk in a rice cooker along with saffron, carraway seeds, coriander seeds, salt and ghee.

• Marinate the chicken in salt and the ginger-garlic paste.

• Place the chopped onions in a large vessel or any flat-bottomed vessel and allow to cook till soft and pink in colour. Put in the chicken, lower the flame, and allow the chicken to cook in it's own juice for 5 to 8 minutes. Then add the ground masala and the water with which you have washed your grinding stone or mixie and taste for salt. Allow the chicken gravy to come to a boil and then simmer, covered with a lid. Add water on the lid. Keep checking the chicken. When the gravy shows signs of drying up add the thick coconut milk, keep putting water on the lid and cook till the chicken is soft and tender. When the chicken is soft, mix it well in the gravy and taste for salt. Remove from the fire.

• In high sided, well-greased vessel, place 3 layers of rice mixed with rose petals, with 2 layers of the chicken and its gravy in-between. Top with the silver vark and cover tightly with foil or a lid and dough, which will plaster the lid and the edges of the vessel together. Place on an iron tava over medium heat for 20 minutes.

Accompaniments:

A Cold Fresh Salad

Beans

Sweet Curd

Sweet Sabudana with Fruits

GRILLED CHICKEN DRUMSTICKS PULAO

- Preparation Time: 30 mins. • Marinating Time: Overnight • Cooking Time: 50 mins.
- Serves: 10

FOR THE RICE AND CHICKEN

450	gms. basmati rice
1	tsp. carraway seeds; 3 bay leaves
20	chicken drumsticks
700	gms. large ripe tomatoes deseeded and skinned
350	gms. baby potatoes boiled and skinned
400	gms. onions finely chopped
2	packets fresh chives
1	cup coriander freshly chopped
2	tbsps. freshly chopped mint
Salt	
Ghee	

FOR THE MASALA

6	green cardamoms seeds only
2	1" pieces cinnamon
15	black peppercorns
1	tbsp. shahjeera
4	mace flowers
1	star anise
8	bedki chillies
8	cloves garlic
1"	fresh ginger

Grind with a little water

½	cup extra fresh chopped coriander
1	tbsp. sugar
Salt	
Pure ghee	

- The previous day grind the masala to a paste. Wash the chicken drumsticks twice and make 3 slashes into the flesh. Rub in salt and then the paste and marinate overnight in the refrigerator.

- The next day barbeque the drumsticks over a coal fire. Rub the chicken slightly with a piece of muslin dipped in pure ghee whilst cooking over the coals. Turn twice on each side and baste with the ghee till tender. Set aside.

- Cook the rice along with salt, 2 tablespoons of pure ghee and the carraway seeds and bay leaves in a rice cooker.

- Place the finely chopped onions in a large, flat-bottomed vessel. Add 3 to 4 tablespoons ghee and cook the onions till pink and transparent. Add the fresh coriander and mint and the barbequed chicken. Add the potatoes after frying them in pure ghee. Mix gently and cook for 5 minutes.

- Cook the pulped tomatoes till thick. Add, sugar and cook for 10 minutes till the sauce thickens. Then add the sauce to the drumsticks, stir and allow to cook for 5 minutes.

- Place the cooked rice in a layer at the bottom of a large pan. Snip the chives with scissors and sprinkle the cut pieces on the rice. Skewer the drumsticks and arrange them on the rice. Cover with the rest of the rice. Sprinkle the remaining chives on the rice and left over gravy on the rice.

Accompaniments:

Onion and pineapple kachumber

Masala mutton

Tomato raita

Moogh dal halwa.

TANDOORI CHICKEN THIGH PULAO SMOTHERED
IN CREAM AND CURD

• Preparation Time: 40 mins. • Cooking Time: 1 hr. • Serves: 8

FOR THE RICE

350	gms. basmati rice
3	star anise
3	large black cardamoms
1	tbsp. ghee
Salt	

FOR THE CHICKEN THIGHS

Marinate them overnight:

12	medium sized chicken thighs
1	cup milk
1½	tsp. freshly ground black peppercorns
1	tbsp. ginger-garlic paste
Salt	

MASALA FOR THE CHICKEN

500	gms. thick curd
200	gms. fresh cream
1	bunch spring onions finely chopped from base upto 6"
6	green chillies deseeded and finely cut
1½	cups coriander freshly cut
2	large green peppers cut into tiny squares
¼	cup coriander extra finely chopped
1	gm. saffron

FOR THE DECORATION

½	cup crimson pomegranate seeds
½	cup golden raisins deep fried

Accompaniments:

A salad of avocados and fresh pineapple

Boondi raita

Hot lemon pickle

• Wash the thighs twice. Cut 3 diagonal slits lightly on the top of each piece. Marinate in salt, ginger-garlic paste, black pepper and one cup milk, overnight in the refrigerator.

• The next day grill the chicken pieces over hot coals. Dab with a piece of muslin dipped in pure ghee. Turn the pieces up and down twice till soft to the touch.

• Take a flat bottomed pan and put in two tablespoons of ghee. Add the spring onions cut julienne and lightly cook over a low flame. Add the coriander, cumin, green chillies, and fry for 4 minutes. Whisk the curd and sprinkle fine salt over it. Whip the cream lightly and sprinkle fine salt over it along with fresh coriander and set aside.

• Heat the saffron over an iron tava or griddle. Mix with your fingers and drop it into the whisked curd. Mix well till the colour runs.

• Cook the rice with the star anise and large black cardamoms along with one tablespoon pure ghee and salt.

• Taste the curd and cream for salt and gently mix into the fried onions. Fold in the barbequed thighs and allow to cook over a very, very low flame for 10 minutes. Mix in the green peppers.

• Take a large high sided pyrex dish or pan. Layer half the rice at the bottom of the pan and pile up the chicken thighs neatly in a layer over the rice. Cover with the remaining rice. Sprinkle the extra coriander over the rice. Cover tightly with foil. Place an iron tava over a medium flame and place the prepared pan on it. Allow to cook on dum for 15 minutes. If using pyrex dish place in an oven at 325⁰ F for 15 minutes.

• Decorate with pomegranate seeds and raisins.

63

PILAN-NO-PULAO (SPRING CHICKEN PULAO)

• Preparation Time: 25 - 35 mins. • Cooking Time: 1½ hours • Serves: 15-20

FOR THE RICE

2	gms. saffron
400	gms. basamati rice
5	bay leaves
150	gms. fried onions
8	cardamom skins
Salt	
Pure ghee	
Oil	

FOR THE GROUND MASALA

16	kashmiri chillies	
1	tbsp. black peppercorns	
2"	piece cinnamon	Grind
7	cloves	together
4	flowers mace	with a
8	green cardamoms seeds	little
	only	water
1	tbsp. broken star anise	
1	tbsp. fennel seeds	
1	cup dried seedless raisins	

FOR THE CHICKEN

6	spring chickens about 400/500 gms.
6	boiled eggs
6	apples
2	large sour limes
500	gms. mutton boti (small pieces)
500	gms. onions finely chopped
350	gms. fried onions
650	gms. tomatoes finely chopped
3	tbsps. garlic and ginger paste

• Wash the chickens 3 times. Cut the dukes nose and stitch up the cavity with a strong white cord.

• Wash the rice 2 to 3 times and cook in a rice cooker with the saffron, fried onions, bay leaves, cardamom skins, salt and pure ghee till each grain is separated and tender. Set aside.

• Marinate the chickens with the garlic and ginger paste and place in a cool area. Rub the sour limes over the chickens.

• Place the chopped onions and some ghee in a large open mouthed vessel and cook on medium heat. When the onions soften add the mutton botis and cook till red. Add the ground masala and the chopped tomatoes. Cover and allow to cook in its own juice for 10 minutes. Transfer to a pressure cooker and cook till soft.

• Wash the raisins and add them to the cooked rice and stir in gently.

• Chop, peel and core the apples and cut them into neat pieces. Peel and cut the boiled eggs. Mix both these, apples and eggs, along with the boti into a clean vessel. Place on a low heat and dry the gravy till you have a thick mixture.

1. *Parsi Sés with a Pyramid Ladva (for Pregnancy occasion)*

2. *Kesar Kalia aur Zaffrani Pulao*

3. *Gulab Jamuns sprinkled with Nuts*

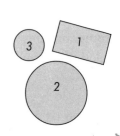

- Open the throat cavity and fill the chickens with the boti mixture. Then fold the throat flap and the neck portion into the cavity and stitch neatly with thick white thread. Lay each chicken on a wooden block, breast side up. Thrust a long, strong, threaded needle near the knee joint, push it through the bird and out at the other knee joint. Tie up the wings neatly at the back and the legs in the front.

- Take a large kadhai or any other large pan. Fill it half way with oil. When hot, lower each chicken — one at a time — and fry till deep golden red. Then place them in a large open-mouthed vessel, arranged neatly, along with two litres of hot water or preferably two litres of chicken stock, and cook the chickens till tender. Add the squeezed lime pieces to the pan. If using water add some salt to taste.

- Heat the saffron rice and raisins and spread over a silver salver. Arrange the stuffed chickens neatly on it. Sprinkle with fried onions and serve.

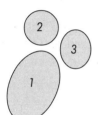

1. *Pilan-no-Pulao*
2. *Chilli-Banana-Boondi Raita*
3. *Mango Pickle in Oil*

SHREDDED CHICKEN PULAO WITH PINEAPPLE RINGS

• Preparation Time: 15 mins. • Cooking Time: 50 mins. • Serves: 6-8

FOR THE RICE

400	gms. basmati rice
2	bay leaves
4	cloves
½	tsp. mustard seeds
½	tsp. coriander seeds
½	tsp. cumin seeds
1	red pepper cut julienne
1	golden pepper cut julienne
1	green pepper cut julienne
200	gms. broccoli cut into fine slices
Salt	
Olive oil	

FOR THE CHICKEN

1	kg whole chicken
1	can pineapple slices
6	spring onion cut in fine circles
1 +	2thick stalks celery cut julienne
2	tbsp. fresh thyme
2	tbsp. fresh sage
2	tbsp. fresh basil
6	green chillies deseeded
1	tbsp. black pepper powder
1 +	1½ tbsp minced fresh ginger
1	tbsp. minced fresh garlic
6	canned red cherries

• Wash the chicken twice inside out. Salt it. Place the chicken to boil in hot slightly salted water. Add the extra one tablespoon ginger and one celery stalk cut julienne. Cook till the meat falls off the chicken bones. Shred the chicken into thick pieces. Cool, strain and reserve the soup as stock for some other dish.

• Wash the rice twice. Add two tablespoons of olive oil to a small vessel. Heat it and then add the bay leaves, cloves, cumin, coriander and mustard seeds. Allow the seeds to pop and add the washed rice and salt and stir for five minutes. Transfer to a rice cooker, add sufficient water and cook till tender. Cool.

• Take a wok and add 3 tablespoons of olive oil. Heat the oil and add the ginger garlic and stir for three minutes. Add the chicken shreds and green chillies and stir for five minutes. Sprinkle with the black pepper powder. Mix well and add the sliced spring onions, celery, thyme, sage and basil and reduce the flame to low.

• Gently sauté the peppers lightly in one tablespoon olive oil in a frying pan. Keep warm.

• Reserve six slices of the canned pineapple for decoration. Chop the rest of the slices into half inch pieces. Reserve the canned syrup.

• After cooking the chicken and herbs for five minutes gently add the rice to the wok and stir gently so the rice grains don't break. Sprinkle a little of the syrup on the rice and add the chopped pineapple pieces. Stir well. Place the hot rice on a dish and surround it with the 6 pineapple slices. Place a cherry in the centre of each slice.

Accompaniments:

Hot tomato gravy or a plain veg. curry

Buttered garlic prawns or pan-fried fish with sesame

AMIRI MURGH PASANDE KA PULAO

FOR THE RICE

2	gms. saffron
700	gms. basmati rice
1	tsp. carraway seeds
Salt	
Ghee	

FOR THE CHICKEN PASANDAS

1500 gms.	whole large chicken breasts
½	tbsps. ginger garlic paste
6	red kashmiri chillies ground into paste
3	large onions chopped fine
Salt	
Ghee	

FOR THE GROUND MASALA (No. 1)

1	tbsp. fennel	
1	tbsp. coriander seeds	
1	tbsp. poppy seeds	
1	tsp. cumin	
1	large pod garlic cloves	Grind in ½ cup of water
10	black peppercorns	
½"	piece cinnamon	
2	cloves	
½	tsp. dried ginger powder	

200	gms. cashew paste (No. 2)	Grind
2	deseeded green chillies	

FOR THE DECORATION

1	green capsicum	Cut the peppers into squares or diamonds dipped into hot oil and removed within one minute
1	red pepper	
1	golden pepper	

• Cook the rice with the carraway seeds, salt and 1 tablespoon ghee in a rice cooker.

• Cut each large chicken breast into 2 pieces. Wash thrice and marinate for 1 hour in the ginger garlic paste, red chilli paste and salt.

• Chop the onions finely. Put them in a large vessel with 2 tablespoons of ghee. Place over medium fire and cook till soft and pink. Add ground masala No. 1 and stir well for 7 minutes. Lower the flame and add the chicken pasandas and stir up and down gently for 7 to 10 minutes. Allow the chicken to cook in its own juice. Then add 2 cups of water, reduce the flame to its lowest and cook the chicken till tender. Cover with a tight fitting lid and put water on it.

• When the chicken is tender, mix the cashew paste No. 2 with a cup of water and add to the cooked chicken and bring to a single boil. Taste for salt and remove from the fire.

• Place the hot rice in a dish and arrange the pasandas on top along with its thick gravy. Decorate with square or diamond shaped pieces of red, green and golden, lightly fried peppers. Serve at once.

BADAM KISMIS MALAI BHARELI MURGHI NO PULAO
(Cream and dried fruit stuffed Chicken Pulao)

• Preparation Time: 30 mins. • Cooking Time: 1 hour • Serves: 10

FOR THE RICE

3	gms. saffron
1	kg. basmati rice
300	gms. potatoes peeled cut into small cubes
100	gms. raisins
1	carrot cut into cubes
400	gms. sweet corn (green giant)
4	spring onions (only white portion) chopped julienne
5	green cardamoms crushed
6	cloves lightly bruised
Salt	
Ghee	

FOR THE CHICKENS

10	whole spring chickens
1½	tbsps. ginger garlic paste
400	gms. yogurt
Salt	
Ghee	

FOR THE CHICKEN STUFFING

20	boiled eggs kept whole
100	gms. almonds toasted and crushed
100	gms. pistachios toasted and crushed
100	gms. green peas boiled
400	gms. cream
1	cup fresh coriander finely chopped
½	cup fresh mint finely chopped
6	green chillies deseeded and chopped
2	tsps. sugar
1	tsp. black pepper powder
1½	tsps. crushed fresh ginger
2	tbsps. butter
1	large needle and white cord
10	2" inch pieces celery
Juice of 2 sour limes	
Salt	

• Cook the rice with all its ingredients in the pressure cooker.

• Wash all the chickens inside out 3 times. Marinate in salt, ginger garlic paste and yoghurt and keep in a cool place.

• Make the stuffing by combining all the ingredients in a thali, mixing well with butter. Taste for salt. Divide the mixture into 10 portions and stuff the chickens with it. Stitch up both ends of the chickens.

• Place one large pan with ghee — atleast 2 cups — heat, and place the chickens inside, covering immediately so you don't get spattered with hot ghee. After the crackling (because of the yogurt) has stopped turn the stitched chickens so that they get evenly browned. Add the celery and 2 litres water. Cover and cook over low fire till the flesh is tender. Lightly sprinkle fine salt over the chickens. Cover with a large lid and add water on it. Whenever necessary add the hot water on the lid which you must immediately replace. Dry up the soup till only a cup or two is left.

• Take a large vessel with a matching lid. Grease the bottom and sides and place half the rice at the bottom. Arrange the birds in a neat circle in its centre. Cover with the remaining rice and gravy from the chicken. Seal the lid tightly with dough and place over a large iron tava over medium heat for half an hour.

• Serve with a sweet, sour and hot tomato gravy, boiled egg and tomato salad, coconut chutney and an almond and saffron kheer.

BLACK PEPPER BEAUTIES

• Preparation Time: 20 mins. • Cooking Time: 50 mins.-1 hour • Serves: 6

FOR THE RICE

400	gms. basmati rice
150	gms. peeled cubed potatoes
2	onions sliced deep fried
1	cup broken cashewnuts fried
10	crushed black peppercorns
Salt	
Ghee	

FOR THE BLACK PEPPERS

9	large black peppers their stems carefully removed, deseeded and stem replaced
Salt	
Butter	

FOR THE STUFFING

6	chicken breasts cut into cubes
½	litre milk
250	gms. cheese
2	tbsps. maida
2	tbsps. celery finely chopped
2	green chillies deseeded and minced
1	tsp. ginger garlic paste
3	tbsps. butter
Salt	

FOR THE DECORATION

Carrot curls

• Cook the rice along with the fried onions, cubed potatoes, cashewnuts, crushed peppercorns, salt and ghee.

• Wash the chicken breasts and marinate in the ginger garlic paste and salt for half an hour. Place in a large sauce pan along with 1 tablespoon of butter and allow to cook for 7 minutes over a low flame. Add half a cup of water and cook till the chicken becomes very soft.

• Make a roux or white sauce with the remaining butter and maida. Cook for 5 minutes and add the milk and cook till creamy. Add the cheese and taste for salt. Mix in the cooked chicken, celery and green chillies. Cook for 5 minutes and remove from the fire. Stuff the black peppers and replace their lids. Grease an aluminium tray or pyrex dish well with extra butter. Pour a little warm water, about ¾ cup and place the black peppers in it and bake in a preheated oven at 350°F for 40-45 minutes until the peppers become soft.

• Place the hot rice on a flat dish and arrange the peppers neatly upon it. Decorate with the carrot curls.

Accompaniments:

Green and Red Leafed Salad with Avocado
Cold, Chilled Lagan Custard

SHAHI BADAM AUR MALAI KA PULAO

FOR THE RICE

500   gms. basmati rice
1½   litres milk + ½ cup milk
½   litre thick coconut milk
2   potatoes peeled and cut into cubes
3   bay leaves
4   green cardamoms crushed
4   drops rose essence
Salt
Ghee

FOR THE CHICKEN

400   gms. thick malai or cream from milk
1   kg. boneless chicken
1½   tbsps. ginger garlic paste
Salt

FOR THE MASALA WITH ALMONDS

1   cup unsalted cashewnuts
1   cup almonds boiled skinned
8   green chillies deseeded
½   cup mint leaves
1½   cups fresh coriander chopped
1   tbsp. coriander seeds broiled
½   tbsp. sesame seeds broiled
½   tbsp. poppy seeds broiled
2   tsps. sugar

} Grind in water

FOR THE DECORATION

4   boiled eggs halved
4   sheets silver vark

• Cook the rice with all its ingredients except rose essence.

• Marinate the boneless chicken in salt and ginger garlic paste for an hour.

• Heat 3 tablespoons ghee in a vessel and when hot, lower the flame and add the ground masala and mix vigorously for 5 minutes. Do not allow to get red. Add the boneless chicken and stir for at least 5 minutes and simmer on a low flame for 7 minutes. Add the water with which you have washed the mixie or grinding stone, cook for 7 more minutes. Gradually add a cup of water and allow the chicken to become tender. When almost all the water has dried up, slowly whisk the cream with a fork and add it to the chicken. Stir well, and cover with a lid and add water on the lid. Lower the flame and simmer for 10 more minutes.

• Divide the rice and the chicken both into two portions. Grease a large vessel.

• Add rose essence to half a cup of milk and sprinkle over the rice. Place a layer of chicken at the bottom, top with rice, again place a layer of chicken and top it with a layer of rice. Decorate the top with the halved eggs and the silver vark. Cover with aluminium foil or a lid and dough and place on an iron tava over a medium flame for 20 minutes.

Accompaniments:

A mild Curry or Dal
Pumpkin Raita
Mixed Vegetable Pickle
Malpuas

ARJUMAND BANOO KI KHWAHEESH

• Preparation Time: 40 mins • Cooking Time: 1 hour • Serves: 8-10

Arjumand Banoo will live forever in the hearts of the people who visit the Taj Mahal at Agra. As long as this physical world survives her memory will survive. She was the wife of Shah Jahan, the grandson of the great Moghul, Akbar. He was madly in love with his wife and she lived for seventeen years with him in luxury and in terror, in comfort and in hardship. She accompanied him to war and was with him when he rose against his father and Noor Jahan and preferred to accept the hospitality of his Rajput generals. At these times she must have been tormented by the heat of the desert and yearned for the vale of Kashmir, its gardens, fruits and flowers and its cool climate. In seventeen years, she presented Shah Jahan with fourteen children and died young whilst delivering her last child.

This recipe is written as a tribute to her.

FOR THE RICE

2	gms. saffron
800	gms. basmati rice — Laal Killa or Sadhu Brand

4	green cardamoms	To be lightly crushed and placed in a potli
4	cloves	
6	black peppercorns	
2	tbsps. coriander seeds broiled	
1"	piece cinnamon	
2	mace flowers	

Salt
Ghee

FOR THE STUFFED CHICKEN ROLLS

20	single chicken breasts boneless
400	gms. finely minced mutton
1000	gms. cream
250	gms. almonds boiled skinned ground to a fine paste with water
2	tbsps. ginger juice

2	large onions sliced deep fried	ground to a paste
10	black peppercorns	
1	tsp. coriander seeds	
½	tsp. mace powder	
½	tsp. dill seeds	

• Cook the rice in the normal manner with the potli, water, salt and ghee.

• The potli should be lowered into the prepared rice cooker so that it touches the bottom. The cord should extend out of the cooker so you can place it on the table and weigh it down with any heavy object. This is done so that you can easily pull out the potli once the rice is done. Discard it.

• Wash the chicken breasts twice. Lightly pound them so they stretch and become larger — they should not tear. Marinate them in salt and ginger juice and set aside.

• Take the fried onions and grind them along with the peppercorns, coriander seeds, dill seeds and mace powder.

• Place a flat bottomed vessel on a medium to low flame. Add 2 tablespoons of ghee. Add the salt and mince and stir vigorously for 10 minutes. Add a little water at a time and cook till tender. When the mince is tender dry up the juice till only 2 to 3 tablespoons are left. Cool and grind fine on a grinding stone or in a mixie. When the mince has been ground to a paste, grind the fried onion mixture along with it. Set the mixture aside. Taste for salt.

THE EXTRAS FOR THE RICE AND TOPPING

400	gms. best quality creamy salted paneer cut into small cubes and lightly fried in ghee
½	can cherries drained from the syrup and lightly sautéed in ghee
1	cup pistachios boiled sliced and fried
½	cup ruby red pomegranate seeds
4	sheets of silver vark or foil

Accompaniments:

Pomegranate and Potato Raita

Mutton Gravy

Boiled Sour Lime Pickle

Baby Gulabjamuns in Saffron Kheer

- Place each breast piece on a wooden board and spread the mince paste lightly over it. Roll the breast piece from the tail side, tightly. Then tie it with a thin thread so it does not unfurl whilst cooking. Do the same with the rest of the chicken breasts.

- Place 2 tablespoons ghee along with 2 cups of water in a vessel. When the water boils, gently release the thread tied rolls into it. Cook over a low flame till the chicken breasts are tender. Once they are done, beat the cream very lightly, and pour onto the rolls. Sprinkle lightly with salt and cook till you get a thick creamy sauce. Broil the carraway seeds, crush them between the palms of your hands and drop them into the cream sauce. If by any chance your cream sauce curdles take 4 tablespoon of corn flour to 1 small tea cup of water and mix well. Remove the rolls with a spoon with holes and set them aside. Mix the cornflour and water into the cream sauce and cook till smooth. Then put back the rolls after removing the thread with a sharp scissor. Replace on the stove and put in the almond paste. Stirring gently, cook for 10 more minutes.

TO ASSEMBLE THE PULAO

- Place the rice in a thali and gently mix in half the sliced pistachios and all the fried paneer. Divide the rice into 2 portions — two-third and one-third.

- Take a flat bottomed vessel. Grease it well and place ²/₃ of the rice in the vessel. Gently spread out the creamy gravy and the chicken rolls on top of the rice and cover with the left over rice. Cover with a lid and dough. Place on an iron griddle over a medium flame for 25 minutes.

- Serve on a silver salver. Remove the rice and chicken carefully with a porcelain quarter plate and sprinkle over the rest of the pistachios and pomegranate seeds. Then stud the rice with the cherries and cover with the silver foil.

EAST INDIAN CHICKEN PULAO

• Preparation Time: 20 mins. • Cooking Time: 1 hour • Serves: 6-8

East Indians are Hindus who lived on the West Coast of India. They were "Brahmins, Prabhus, Charkalshish, Katris, Bhandaris, Kunbis, Khumbhars, Nhavis, Dhobis, Kolis and Chamars who were converted to Christianity by the Portuguese and were divided in five cultural groups". Most of the East Indians worked closely with the Portuguese and the English and became greatly westernized. They built many churches and favoured western types of Architecture whilst building their homes. These people became very devout Catholics.

FOR THE RICE

500	gms. long grained rice
1	pod large garlic
1½"	piece ginger
3	large onions
3	bay leaves
Salt	
Refined oil or Pure ghee	

FOR THE CHICKEN

1200	gms. small pieces of chicken
1½	tbsps. ginger-garlic paste
500	gms. tomatoes skinned
200	gms. mixed vegetables like frenchbeans, carrots, potatoes cut julienne
6	cloves
6	green cardamoms lightly crushed
2"	piece of cinnamon
10	black peppercorns lightly crushed
1	tsp. carraway seeds
2	stalks celery cut into 2" pieces
Oil or ghee	

Accompaniments:

Mince Pattice

Lettuce and Beet Salad

Stewed Apples with Caramel Cream

• Place a large frying pan on the stove with ½ cup of pure ghee. When hot add the onions cut into fine slices, the ginger and garlic cut julienne and cook stirring all the time till soft and pink. Add the bay leaves and fry for 2 minutes. Wash the rice twice and add it to the fried onion mixture along with salt. Cook for 5 minutes and place in the rice cooker. Add sufficient water to cook it till ¾ cooked.

• Take 3 tablespoons of oil and place it in a large vessel on medium heat. When hot add all the whole, dried spices and stir for 2 to 3 minutes.

• Wash the chicken before cooking the rice and marinate it in salt and the ginger garlic paste for atleast half an hour. Put it in the hot oil containing the cloves, cardamoms, cinnamon and peppercorns. Add the cut celery and lower the flame and cook for 5 minutes. Add the skinned tomatoes and cook on low heat for 7 minutes. When soft add the cut vegetables and taste for salt. Add 2 cups of water and cook over a very low heat till chicken is tender. Place a tight lid on the vessel and add water on the lid. Keep stirring the chicken and checking it for tenderness. When necessary add the hot water from the lid. When the chicken is ready, mix the rice and put it on top of the cooked chicken. Cover with the same lid and cook for 35 minutes on very low heat.

PARSI TATRELI (FRIED AND ROASTED) MARGHI-NO-PULAO

• Preparation Time: 25 mins. • Cooking Time: 55 mins. • Serves: 4-6

FOR THE RICE

750 gms. basmati rice
2 gms. saffron
1 pinch saffron colour
1 tsp. carraway seeds
6 allspice corns
Salt
1 tbsp. ghee

FOR THE CHICKEN

1200 gms. large chicken cut into small pieces
2 tsps. ginger-garlic paste
4 large onions finely chopped
4 large potatoes skinned and each cut into 8 pieces
3 tomatoes skinned and finely chopped
200 gms. thick curd
Salt
Refined peanut oil

FOR THE GROUND MASALA

10 large kashmiri chillies deseeded
12 peppercorns
1" cinnamon stick
1 tsp. star anise broken pieces
½ tsp. cardamom seeds
½ tsp. shahjeera seeds
2 mace flowers

} Grind fine in a little water

FOR THE DECORATION

4 boiled eggs quartered
1 large capsicum cut julienne
½ cup fried cashewnuts

• Cook the rice into 2 portions. In one portion add the saffron, pinch of saffron colour, salt and ½ tablespoon ghee. Cook the second portion with the carraway seeds, allspice corns, salt and ½ a tablespoon ghee.

• Place oil in a karhai and when hot, deep fry the potatoes, salted, till golden brown. Take a vessel and place 2 tablespoons of the potato fried oil, into it. Add the finely chopped onions, place on medium heat and cook till golden brown.

• Wash the chicken pieces, marinate in salt and the ginger-garlic paste and toss them onto the golden brown onions in the vessel. Lower the flame and mix the pieces well and allow to fry in the onion mixture till the pieces are dried and red. Add the ground masala and stir for 3 minutes and add the grinding stone water. Cook for 5 minutes till the chicken makes a rustling sound. Whisk the curd and add to the chicken; add tomatoes.

• Cover and keep over a very, very low flame and cook till soft. Taste for salt. If necessary add ½ cup of warm water twice so the chicken does not burn.

• Place the white rice in a large vessel and top it with the chicken. Cover the chicken with the saffron rice. Put the vessel on an iron tava on medium heat for 25 minutes.

• Remove on a silver salver and cover with fried potatoes, quartered eggs, julienne capsicums and fried cashew nuts.

Accompaniments:

Apple, Raisin and Green Chilli Chutney
Spring Onions with Avocado slices
Carrot Halwa with Cream

PULAO MURGH KANDAHARI

· Preparation Time: 20 mins. · Cooking Time: 1 hour · Serves: 8-10

FOR THE RICE

2	gms.	saffron
600	gms.	basmati rice
3		onions sliced and deep fried
2"		pieces cinnamon
4		green cardamoms crushed
3		cloves
Salt		
Ghee		

FOR THE CHICKEN

8	large chicken breasts each cut into three chunks
500	gms. thick cream
500	gms. thick yogurt
300	gms. chopped onions, sliced deep fried and crushed to pulp
Salt	
Ghee	

FOR THE GROUND MASALA

200	gms. broken cashewnuts broiled	
3	red kashmiri chillies deseeded	
3	cloves	Grind to a pulp with ½ cup water
3	cardamoms seeds only	
½	tbsp. cumin	
1	tbsp. poppy seeds	
1	pod garlic	
2"	fresh ginger	

FOR THE DECORATION

½ cup red pomegranate seeds

· Cook the rice with the saffron, onions, cinnamon, cardamom, cloves, salt and a tablespoon of ghee in a rice cooker.

· Place the fried onions in a mixie or on a grinding stone till you get a pulp. Place it in a large vessel over medium heat. Wash and salt the chicken pieces and cook them along with the crushed onions over a low heat. Cover and add water on the lid and cook for 15 minutes. Add 1 cup of water at a time and cook till tender. Dry off the water and add the finely ground masala and its water and stir the chicken for 10 minutes. Add the yogurt and stir for another 10 minutes. Then add the cream and stir gently for another 10 minutes. Taste for salt.

· Place half the rice in a vessel and cover it with the chicken gravy. Cover with the remaining rice. Place burning coals in a small vessel in the centre of the rice and add a teaspoon of ghee to the coals. Quickly cover the vessel with a lid and dough and cook on an iron tava for 30 minutes. Decorate with the pomegranate seeds.

Accompaniments:

Thick gravied Mutton Kofta dish

Curd with Herbs

Green Cucumbers, Peaches and Pears

Fig Ice-cream with walnuts

BATER (QUAILS) KA LAJAWAB PULAO

• Preparation Time: 35-45 mins. • Marinating Time: 2 hours • Cooking Time: 50 mins. • Serves: 6

Before India gained Independence, Maharajas and the Indian aristocrats, alongwith the British officials went on tiger, wild boar hunting and bird shoots. The birds which were hunted were those which used to fly during breeding times to northern Indian ponds and lakes. The favourites were green coloured mallards, large geese, quails (baters) tiny birds, partridges and various types of pheasants. Today some of these are still found in the wild and are offered to the rich for consumption. But a better way to eat these birds is to order them from special breeders. You have to specify the weight of the bird when ordering. It's very small so you must cook at least two quails for each person you invite for dinner.

FOR THE RICE

1	gm. saffron
800	gms. basmati rice
2	onions sliced deep fried
½	tsp. carraway seeds
4	bay leaves
Salt	
Ghee	

FOR THE QUAILS

12	quails roughly 300 gms. each
3	large onions finely chopped
3	large tomatoes finely chopped
300	gms. thick curd
500	gms. cream
1	gm. saffron

FOR THE MASALA

1½"	piece ginger
6	kashmiri chillies deseeded
12	black peppercorn
1"	piece cinnamon
2	mace flowers
2	cloves
1	star anise
1	tbsp. poppy seeds
1	tbsp. coriander seeds broiled
Salt	
Ghee	

Grind to a fine paste with ½ cup of water. Retain water after washing the grinding stone.

• Wash the birds twice, inside and out. Salt them and set aside.

• Grind the masala very fine and apply it to the birds. Lightly whisk the curd and pour over the birds, turning them up and down 2 to 3 times so that all of them are well coated with the curd. Allow to marinate for 2 hours.

• When the marination period is over, cook the rice along with the onions, carraway seeds, bay leaves, salt, saffron and 1½ tablespoons of ghee, in a rice cooker.

• Take a large flat bottomed, rectangular pan or large vessel. Put in 1 cup of pure ghee, add the onions and place over medium heat and cook till soft. Add the tomatoes and cook till soft and pulpy and then arrange the quails and stir them well in the tomato mixture. Cook for 10 minutes stirring gently now and then. Pour all the remaining marinade over the birds, close lightly, and cook till soft. You may have to add some water to make the quails very tender. Just sprinkle a little water at a time on the birds so as not to lose the taste.

• Steep the saffron in half a cup of boiling water. Whisk the cream and add to the pan. Macerate the saffron in the water and add it on top of the

FOR THE DECORATION

6	hard boiled quail eggs cut into half
100	gms. seedless raisins fried
100	gms. almonds boiled skinned fried whole

cream. Cook for 7 more minutes. Remove from the fire.

- Place the hot rice on a large silver salver and cover it with the quails along with the remaining gravy. Decorate by topping the birds with half-cut quails eggs and the fried raisins and almonds.

FRESH APRICOT AND CROQUETTE PULAO

• Preparation Time: 25 mins. • Cooking Time: 50 mins. • Serves: 6-8

FOR THE RICE

1	gm. saffron
500	gms. basmati rice
2	onions sliced and fried
3	allspice leaves
½	tsp. carraway seeds
10	black peppercorns
1	tbsp. ghee
Salt	

FOR THE SOUP

1	kg. mutton bones
½	tbsp. coriander seeds broiled
4	green cardamoms crushed
2	cloves crushed
1"	fresh ginger crushed
6	fresh garlic cloves crushed
Salt	

FOR THE GRAVY

1	tbsp. ginger-garlic finely ground
2	large onions finely chopped
4	large tomatoes skinned, finely chopped
Salt	
Sunflower oil	

GROUND MASALA FOR THE GRAVY

10	kashmiri chillies deseeded	
½	tbsp. fennel	
½	tbsp. black peppercorns	
½	tbsp. cinnamon crushed	Grind in ¼ cup of water
½	tbsp. black cardamoms crushed	
½"	piece turmeric	
½	tsp. mace	
½	tsp. nutmeg	

• Cook the rice with the saffron, fried onions, allspice leaves, carraway seeds, peppercorns, salt and ghee in a rice cooker.

• Wash the mutton bones twice in cold water. Crack the nali bones. Place all the bones along with 5 cups of water, salt, the coriander seeds, cardamoms, cloves, fresh ginger and garlic into a pressure cooker and cook for half an hour. Open the cooker and pour the soup and the bones in a large vessel and allow to simmer for half an hour till the soup has been reduced to two cups. Strain the soup through a fine mesh colander into a clean small vessel.

• Take a flat vessel and place ½ tablespoon of ghee and the finely chopped onions in it and cook them over a medium flame till soft and pink. Add the tomatoes and cook them till they are soft and pulpy. Then add the ground masala and cook over a very low fire for 10 minutes. When the masala emits a fragrant aroma and is well cooked add the strained soup and allow the mixture to simmer.

• Whilst the bones are cooking, place the mince in a thali. Squeeze all the water from the bread and add it to the mince along with 2 eggs, chopped chillies, coriander, mint, spring onions, garam masala, salt, chilli, turmeric and amchoor powder. Mix and knead the mince mixture with both your hands after wetting them until you have a smooth ball of mince. Tear pieces of the mince and shape into thick, rectangular croquette shapes atleast 1½" long and about ¾" in thickness.

• Whisk the remaining eggs and dip the croquettes in them, roll them in the breadcrumbs and deep

FOR THE CROQUETTES

700 gms. fine mince
9 slices stale bread soaked in water
10 sweet green chillies deseeded and finely chopped
1½ cups coriander freshly chopped
2 tbsps. mint freshly chopped
6 spring onions freshly chopped
2 tbsps. garam masala
1 tbsp. chilli powder
½ tbsp. turmeric powder
½ tsp. amchoor powder
6 eggs
Breadcrumbs
Salt
Sunflower oil

FOR THE APRICOTS

10 fresh apricots skinned stoned and halved
½ cup sugar
1 cup water
½ tsp. allspice corns

fry in a karai in hot boiling oil till golden brown. Lift them when cooked and place them in a colander to drain the oil.

- Poach the skinned apricots in 1 cup of water and ½ a cup of sugar till soft. Add them and the fried mince croquettes to the simmering masala gravy and keep on the fire for 5 minutes.

- Layer the rice, gravy-apricots-croquettes in a large vessel. Cover it and place over a tava for 15 minutes before bringing it to the table.

Accompaniments:

Fried chicken livers and chicken tikkas

A salad of red radish, avocado slices, and endive lettuce in lime juice

Cold sweet curd

Cold dark gulabjamuns in a creamy, ivory coloured rabri

RIBBON RICE PULAO

• Preparation Time: 1 hour • Cooking Time: 1 hour • Serves: 10-12

FOR THE RICE

900 gms. basmati rice
3 onions sliced and fried
Salt
Ghee

FOR THE RICE

For the **jalebi pulao** you will need prawn patia
For the **green pulao** you will need coconut chutney
For the **white pulao** you will need sweet and sour mince with black currants.

FOR THE PRAWN PATIA

700	gms.	prawns skinned deveined twice washed
300	gms.	onions finely chopped
300	gms.	tomatoes finely chopped
1		cup coriander finely chopped
3		sprigs curry leaves
½		cup grated jaggery

Salt
Peanut Oil

FOR THE PRAWN GROUND MASALA

12	kashmiri chillies	
1	pod garlic	Grind in
10	black peppercorns	½ cup
1	tbsp. cumin seeds	sugarcane
½	tsp. mustard seeds	vinegar

• TO COOK RICE

In a rice cooker cook 300 gms. washed rice with ¹/₃ the fried onions, a pinch of jalebi colour, salt and ½ tablespoon of ghee.

The 300 gms. of green rice should be cooked with ¹/₃ fried onions, ¼ teaspoon of green colour, salt and ½ tablespoon of ghee.

The white rice should be cooked plain with ¹/₃ the fried onion, salt and ½ tablespoon of ghee.

• TO COOK PRAWN PATIA

Heat ½ to ¾ cup of peanut oil in a medium sized vessel. Add the onions and curry sprigs and cook till soft. Add the finely ground masala and stir over a low fire till red. Add the prawns and cook till soft in the vinegar. Add ½ cup of water only if necessary. Add the tomatoes and coriander and cook till soft. Add the jaggery, cook for a few more minutes, taste for salt and cover.

1. *Kheema Malai Pulao*
2. *Paneer in Masala Gravy*
3. *Bombay Potatoes*
4. *Purees*
5. *Lacchedar Rabri with sliced Pistachios*

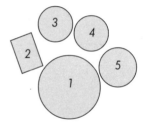

FOR THE COCONUT CHUTNEY

1	large grated coconut	
½	pod garlic cloves	
½	tbsp. cumin seeds	Grind
6-8	green chillies deseeded	very fine
2-3	cups coriander leaves chopped	with ½ a cup of
1	tbsp. sugar	water
3	sour limes with their juice squeezed	

Salt to taste

After the chutney is ground well, add one cup of cold water, mix and set aside.

FOR THE SWEET AND SOUR MINCE

700	gms. mince
½	tbsp. ginger-garlic paste
3	onions chopped fine
3	large tomatoes chopped fine
1	tbsp. garam masala
1½	tsps. chilli powder
1	tsp. turmeric powder
1	cup coriander chopped
½	cup sugarcane vinegar
1	tbsp. sugar

Salt
Peanut oil

TO COOK MINCE

Heat oil in a vessel and add the chopped onions and cook till soft. Add ginger-garlic and salt to the mince and then add to the softened onions. Add the garam masala, chilli powder, chopped tomatoes, turmeric powder, and coriander and cook till soft. Add a cup of water at a time as necessary. Mince must be tender. Wash the black currants and add them as well as the sugar and vinegar and cook till dry.

METHOD

Take an aluminium tray 12" × 6". Spread 3 equal bands of saffron — white — and green rice on the base. Reserve half of all the different coloured rice. On top of the band of saffron rice place the prawn patia and cover with the remaining saffron rice. On top of the white rice lay out the sweet and sour mince and then the remaining white rice on top. On top of the green rice spread the chutney with a palette knife and cover with the remaining rice.

TO DECORATE

Decorate the saffron rice with canned cherries, the white rice with fried black currants and the green rice with boiled green peas.

TO BAKE

Bake in an oven at 350°F for 20 minutes.

Accompaniments:

Dal or Egg Curry
Curd with Melon
Vanilla and Raspberry Ice-cream.

1. *Hyderabadi Bhuna Hua Kheema Pulao*
2. *Malai Sandwich*

DAHIWALLO-KHEEMA-NO-PULAO

• Preparation Time: 20 mins. • Cooking Time: 1 hr. 20 mins. • Serves: 8-10

FOR THE RICE

2	gms. saffron
600	gms. basmati rice
3	black cardamoms
6	allspice corns
2	onions sliced and fried
Salt	
Ghee	

FOR THE KHEEMA

1500	gms. mutton kheema
700	gms. thick creamy curd
4	potatoes peeled and cut into chips
200	gms. baby ladyfingers topped and tailed
300	gms. onions finely chopped
400	gms. tomatoes skinned and chopped
1	cup coriander freshly chopped
½	cup mint freshly chopped
2½	tbsps. ground cumin with 2 green chilies and 15 black peppercorns
1	tbsp. powdered coriander
½	tbsp. powdered carraway seeds
1½	tbsps. ginger-garlic paste
Salt	
Ghee	
Peanut oil	

FOR THE DECORATION

6	boiled eggs halved
3	onions, sliced deep fried
Slivers of almonds	

Accompaniments:

Salad with fruits and cucumbers

Coconut and Coriander Chutney

Mutton Masala

Custard Apple Ice-cream

• Marinate the kheema in salt and the ginger-garlic paste and set aside.

• Cook the rice together with the saffron, black cardamoms, allspice corns, fried onions, salt and ghee in a rice cooker.

• Place the chopped onions along with 1½ cups of pure ghee in a large vessel. Place over medium flame till pink and soft. Then add the mince and fry for seven minutes. Lower the heat and add the ground cumin green chillies and black peppercorns, the powdered coriander and the carraway seeds. Mix for 5 minutes and add the tomatoes and cook for another 5 minutes. Add as much water as necessary, a cup at a time, till the kheema is juicy, soft and tender. Then add in the lightly whisked curd and the fresh coriander and mint. Cover and place over a very low heat and cook till the liquid is almost dried up. Taste for salt.

• Place a karhai, half full with peanut oil on the stove and heat till hot. Drop in the washed, salted baby ladyfingers in batches till green and soft. Drain in a colander. In the same oil, add the salted potato chips and cook till golden brown.

• Place half the rice in a vessel or large pan. Arrange all the kheema over it. Lay the fried ladyfingers and fried chips over the kheema. Cover with the remaining half of the rice. Place a few burning coals in a stainless steel bowl, place a teaspoon of pure ghee on them and immediately cover the kheema pulao with a well-fitting lid. Cover with dough and place over an iron tava for 30 minutes.

• Remove from the fire and open after 10 minutes. Spread out on a salver and decorate with the boiled eggs, fried onions and the almond slivers.

KHEEMA MALAI PULAO

FOR THE RICE

400	gms. basmati rice
2	onions sliced fried
4	bay leaves or allspice leaves
4	green cardamoms bruised
2"	piece cinnamon
½	tsp. jalebi colour
2	tbsps. ghee
Salt	

FOR THE KHEEMA

500	gms. mutton mince
1½	tbsps. ginger-garlic paste
3	large onions finely chopped
3	long green chillies deseeded and chopped
1	cup coriander leaves freshly chopped
6	stalks fresh mint finely chopped
4	large tomatoes skinned and chopped
1	cup thick yogurt
1	cup thick cream
2	tbsps. sugar
Refined peanut oil	
Salt	

FOR THE GROUND MASALA

¼	dry coconut grated	
8	kashmiri chillies deseeded	
10	black peppercorns	Grind in
1	tsp. fennel seeds	¼ cup
3	mace flowers	of water
2	star anise	

FOR THE DECORATION

½	cup black currants fried
6	eggs halved
2	capsicums chopped julienne

• Divide the rice into 2 portions. Cook 1 half with half the onions, jalebi colour, half tablespoon ghee and salt and the other half with one fried onion, bay leaves, green cardamoms, cinnamon, salt and half the ghee, in a pressure cooker. When done, place both the rice in a thali, separately.

• Mix the mutton mince with salt and the ginger-garlic paste. Set aside in a small vessel for half an hour. Place the chopped onions with 2 tablespoons refined peanut oil in a large vessel on medium flame. When hot add the mince and stir vigorously till red. Add the green chillies, coriander, mint, tomatoes and salt and cook over very low fire for 7 minutes.

• Add the ground masala along with the water with which you washed the grinding stone or mixie and cook on very low fire for 15 minutes. If the water dries up keep adding more, 1 cup at a time. Taste for salt. Cover with a good lid and add water on top. Cook till the mince becomes tender and dry. This should be cooked at the same time you cook your rice so your time is saved.

• Take a rectangular silver dish or an aluminium tray, roughly 8"-10" in length and 4"-6" in breadth. Place the white rice at the bottom and cover with the mince. Place the jalebi coloured rice on top. Mix the yogurt in a glass bowl. Add ½ teaspoon salt and 2 teaspoons sugar. Then mix in the cream gently. Sprinkle this mixture over the jalebi rice and top with the boiled eggs, black currants fried and the lightly sautéed green capsicum. cut julienne. Cover with a foil and heat in an oven at 350°F for 10 minutes.

Accompaniments:

Dhansakh Dal

Cucumber, Cumin and Potato Raita

Stuffed Karelas, Banana Fritters and Ice-cream

MOTHER'S CAPSICUM PULAO STUFFED WITH MINCE

• Preparation Time: 45 mins. • Cooking Time: 1 hour 15 mins. • Serves: 10-12

FOR THE RICE

600	gms. basmati rice
2	large onions sliced deep fried
4	bay leaves
2	large brown cardamoms
2	star anise
Salt	
Ghee	

FOR THE CAPSICUMS AND THE MINCE

15	medium sized capsicums
2	onions chopped
750	gms. minced mutton
1	tbsp. ginger-garlic paste
1	tsp. chilli powder
1	tsp. garam masala
1	tsp. turmeric powder
4	large tomatoes skinned and chopped
4	sprig curry leaves
½	cup sugarcane vinegar
½	cup sugar
½	cup black currants
Refined peanut oil	
Salt	

FOR THE RICE TOPPING

4	tomatoes skinned finely chopped
1	tsp. shahjeera coarsely ground
1	tsp. mace coarsely ground
2	cups beaten curd
2	tbsps. fine sugar

Accompaniments:

Stuffed whole chicken

Onion Ring and Avocado Salad

Tamarind Chutney

Malai Kulfi

• Cook the rice along with all the ingredients and 1½ tablespoons of ghee in a rice cooker.

• Wash and dry the capsicums. Cut around the stalks carefully and reserve them. Remove the seeds and keep the stalk lightly on the capsicum.

• Take a large vessel and put in the chopped onions and 1 cup of peanut oil and cook till the onion softens on a medium flame. Add the marinated mince and lower the flame and toss the mince up and down till red. Add the chilli powder, garam masala and turmeric. Stir and add the chopped tomatoes. Cook for 5 minutes and add 2 cups of water and stir over a very low flame. Add water on the cover too. Cook for 30 minutes adding water inside and on top as necessary. Once the mince is tender allow it to dry up. Once it is almost dried add the black currants, vinegar and sugar and stir well and take it off the stove. Taste for salt.

• Sprinkle the capsicums inside out with fine salt. Fill them with the mince and put back the stalks.

• Take a large vessel and add 1 to ½ cup peanut oil and the curry sprigs and allow to heat on a medium stove. When the leaves start spluttering, lower the flame and arrange the capsicums in a circle. Add a pinch of salt over the capsicums and 1½ cups of water, cover and cook on a slow heat till the capsicums are tender.

• Whip the curd lightly. Add the fine sugar, mace, shahjeera and the skinned chopped tomatoes. Mix lightly into the rice. Place half the rice in a large vessel. Make 15 depressions into it. Gently place each capsicum in the depression and fill all the gaps with the rice. Allow the tops and stalks to show. Pour any left over gravy on the rice. Cover with a fitting lid. Apply dough and place for 30 minutes over an iron tava.

MURGH KE KHEEME KA SHAHENSHAHI PULAO

• Preparation Time: 20 mins. • Cooking Time: 1 hour • Serves: 8-10

FOR THE RICE

2	gms. saffron
600	gms. basmati rice
8	green cardamoms crushed
4	bay leaves
1	tsp. shahjeera
6	allspice corns (kababchini)

Salt, Pure ghee

FOR THE CHICKEN KHEEMA

1200	gms. fine chicken mince
3	medium sized onions finely chopped
500	gms. tomatoes skinned deseeded and chopped
2	tbsps. ginger paste
2	tbsps. garlic paste
200	gms. cream

Salt, Pure ghee

FOR THE GROUND MASALA

8	green chillies deseeded	
6	kashmiri dried chillies deseeded	
¼	nutmeg	Grind with ½ cup water
1½"	piece cinnamon	
4	cloves	
2	tbsps. coriander seeds broiled	
1	tbsp. fennel seeds broiled	

FOR THE DECORATION

6	boiled eggs halved
2	cups sliced onions deep fried
100	gms. cashewnuts fried whole salted
100	gms. sliced almonds boiled skinned fried
50	gms. sliced pistachios boiled skinned fried
100	gms. seedless raisins fried
4	sheets silver vark

Rose essence or 1 cup red rose petals

• Add salt, ginger-garlic paste to the chicken mince and allow to marinate for ½ hour.

• Place 2 tablespoons of ghee in a very large vessel. Heat over a medium flame and add the 3 finely chopped onions and allow to cook till pink and soft.

• Add the mince to the onions and keep stirring for 10 minutes over a very low fire. Add the tomatoes the ground masala and stir vigorously for 10 minutes. Add 3 cups of water and cover. Pour water on the lid too and if extra water is needed use this hot water for the mince and replace the water on the lid. Heat the saffron and crumble it in the hot water on the lid and add it to the mince.

• Wash the rice and put it in the rice cooker with all ingredients and 1 tablespoon pure ghee and cook till ¾ done. Add water accordingly.

• Take a non-stick frying pan. Put in some ghee and carefully deep fry, the cashew nuts, almonds, pistachios and raisins.

• When the rice is ¾ cooked, mix it and place it on the mince in the vessel. Sprinkle ½ the nuts and raisins on top of the rice and mix it gently. Lightly beat the cream and sprinkle it on top of the rice. Sprinkle the red rose petals and mix with a fork into the rice. Sprinkle ½ a cup of water and cover the lid tightly with dough. Place on an iron tava over a medium flame and allow to cook for 35 minutes.

• When cooked remove the pulao onto a silver salver with the help of a quarter plate. See that the rice and mince are both integrated. Cover with the halved boiled eggs, nuts, raisins and deep fried onions as well as the silver vark.

Accompaniments:

Sweet mango chutney

A salad of chicken livers and paneer pieces

A light dal

Ripe mangoes with ice-cream

ANDE-KOFTE KA PULAO

● Preparation Time: 20 mins.   ●   Cooking Time: 55 mins.   ●   Serves: 8-10

FOR THE RICE — (A)

300	gms. basmati rice
100	gms. peeled cubed potatoes
1	large onion sliced fried
2	bay leaves
2	(1") piece cinnamon
Salt	
Ghee	

FOR THE RICE — (B)

250	gms. basmati rice
100	gms. peeled cubed potatoes
1	large onion sliced and fried
3	green cardamoms crushed
10	peppercorns
½	tsp. carraway seeds
1	pinch saffron colour

FOR THE KOFTAS

8	boiled eggs halved
500	gms. lean mince
1	tbsp. ginger-garlic paste
1	medium sized onion finely grated
½	cup fresh coriander finely chopped
1	tbsp. mint finely chopped
6	green chillies deseeded finely chopped
1	tbsp. garam masala
1½	tsps. turmeric powder
2	tbsps. yogurt into which mash 3 slices of bread
2	raw eggs for the mince
4-5	raw eggs for frying
Breadcrumbs	
Oil	

FOR THE GRAVY

500	gms. tomatoes, chopped
200	gms. onions, chopped
2	cups mutton soup or water
2	red chillies ground

● Cook the white and coloured rice separately and cool in two separate trays.

● Place the mince in a tray and marinate it in salt and ginger-garlic paste. Add the grated onion, coriander, green chillies, mint, garam masala, turmeric powder, 2 eggs and bread slices soaked in yogurt. Mix well and taste for salt. Divide the mince into 16 portions.

● Wet your hands and place one portion of the mince in your left palm and shape the mince into an oval. Place the halved boiled egg, yolk downwards on the centre of the mince and cover the egg with the mince in an oval form till the egg is thoroughly covered. Press the mince gently so it adheres to the boiled eggs. Roll in breadcrumbs and set aside.

● Roll, cover and shape all the koftas in the above manner and cover with the breadcrumbs. When all the koftas are prepared, half fill a karhai with peanut oil. Beat the raw eggs in a bowl or soup plate. When the oil is hot, lower the flame a little, dip each kofta into the egg mixture and place in the hot oil. Fry a few at a time till golden brown and set aside to cool.

● Place a vessel on medium flame. Put in some oil from the karhai and place the chopped onion into it. Cook till the onion is golden brown. Crush it on a grinding stone and replace it on the fire in the same vessel. Add the soup, ground red chillies, chopped tomato, gram flour, tamarind water, sugar, celery, fennel and powdered shahjeera seeds. Mix well and bring to a quick boil. Taste for salt. When ready set aside to cool.

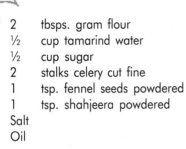

2	tbsps. gram flour
½	cup tamarind water
½	cup sugar
2	stalks celery cut fine
1	tsp. fennel seeds powdered
1	tsp. shahjeera powdered
Salt	
Oil	

- Place the white rice at the base of a well-greased vessel. Spread the gravy over the rice and arrange the fried koftas over the gravy itself. Then cover with the saffron coloured rice. Cover vessel with foil and place it on top of an iron tava over medium flame for 15 minutes.

Accompaniments:

Hot Dal and Kachumber

Sesame Seed and Tamarind Chutney

Payasam

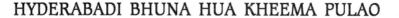

HYDERABADI BHUNA HUA KHEEMA PULAO

• Preparation Time: 10 mins. • Cooking Time: 45-55 mins. • Serves: 6-8

FOR THE RICE

2	gms. saffron
450	gms. basmati rice
3	bay leaves
1"	cinnamon stick
½	tsp. shahjeera
10	black peppercorns
Salt	
Ghee	

FOR THE MINCE

750	gms. mutton mince
300	gms. onions finely chopped
500	gms. tomatoes
2	tsps. garam masala
2	tsps. red chilli powder
1½	tsps. turmeric powder
1½	tsps. cumin coarsely ground
½	tsp. mustard coarsely ground
1	tbsp. fresh ginger crushed
2	tbsp. fresh garlic crushed
½	bunch coriander leaves
6	green chillies deseeded chopped
¼	cup fresh mint leaves chopped
2	bunches fresh khatta bhaji chopped fine
1	bunch dill (suva) bhaji chopped fine
2	sprigs curry leaves
Juice of 2 sour limes	
Salt	
Ghee	

EXTRAS

Hot charcoal in a katori and some ghee

• Prepare the rice with all its ingredients in the rice cooker.

• Cook the chopped onions in 3 tablespoons of ghee till soft and pink. Add the curry leaves.

• Marinate the mince in salt and the crushed ginger and garlic and add to the cooked onions and stir non–stop for 7 minutes so that no lumps form. Add the garam masala, chilli powder, turmeric, cumin and mustard. Lower the flame and add the tomatoes and cover with a lid. Place water on the lid and keep adding the hot water until the mince is tender.

• Wash the khatta bhaji and dill 3 times and chop finely. Sprinkle fine salt on it and add it to the cooked mince and keep stirring it for 5 to 7 minutes till the bhaji is cooked but is not black in appearance. Stir in the chopped coriander leaves, mint, chillies and the juice of 2 sour limes and remove immediately from the fire.

• Portion the rice into 2 and place one half on the base of a well-greased vessel. Then place all the cooked mince on top and cover with the remaining rice.

• Place a stainless steel katori filled with live red hot coals in the middle of the rice. Pour some ghee — half a tablespoon, over the coals and cover the vessel quickly with a lid and dough. Place on an iron tava over medium heat for 30 minutes. Remove the katori before serving the pulao.

Accompaniments:

Hot Masala Dal

Sweet and Sour Mango Pickle

Green Coriander Chutney with Papads

Custard Apple Ice-cream

MANGO PULAO WITH BLACK PEARLS

• Preparation Time: 25 mins. • Cooking Time: 40 mins. • Serves: 10

6 large malgoba mangoes. They need not be ripe

FOR THE RICE

500	gms. basmati rice
2	gms. saffron
3	large onions fried
3	bay leaves
4	cloves
6	crushed green cardamoms
2"	piece cinnamon
10	black peppercorns
1	tsp. coriander seeds broiled
1	tsp. cumin seeds broiled

FOR THE BABY MEAT BALLS

250	gms. mutton mince
150	gms. mashed potato
2	slices bread soaked in water
6	green chillies deseeded and cut fine
½	teacup fresh coriander chopped
1	tsp. turmeric powder
1	tsp. chilli powder
1½	tsps. dhansakh masala
2	tsps. ginger-garlic paste
3	eggs
Bread crumbs	

FOR THE MEAT BALL GRAVY

6	large ripe malgoba mangoes
4	onions finely chopped
2	onions sliced and golden fried
4	very large tomatoes skinned deseeded and finely chopped
2	tbsp. Prakash's garam masala
1	tbsp. sugar
½	cup fresh coriander finely chopped
Salt	
Oil	
Pure ghee	

• Wash the rice 3 times. Place in a vessel along with the fried onions, whole spices, salt and 75 gms. pure ghee. Cook in a rice cooker.

• In a thali mash together the mutton mince, ginger-garlic paste, mashed potatoes, green chillies, coriander, salt, turmeric, chilli and dhansakh masala powders. Mix well. Mix in the 2 slices of bread soaked in water. Dampen both hands and make tiny little balls. Cover with bread crumbs. Heat a karhai of oil. When hot, dip the little balls in beaten eggs and fry till golden brown. Place in a colander.

• Peel the mangoes and cut the 2 cheeks and the sides of the mango stone into 1" cubed pieces. Sprinkle sugar and place in a cool place.

• Cook the finely chopped onions in 100 gms. of pure ghee till pink and soft. Add the finely cut tomatoes and allow the gravy to become soft and pulpy. Add Prakash's garam masala and stir for 5 minutes. Gently add the mango pieces. Do not stir. Shake the vessel from side to side by holding it with 2 kitchen napkins. Cover and place on very low flame for 10 minutes.

• Take a tall medium sized vessel and place some rice at the bottom. Then place the mangoes and meat balls in gravy. Arrange several layers and cover the last with the fried onions and fresh coriander. Cover tightly with foil and keep over a low flame for 5-10 minutes.

Accompaniments:

Hot and sweet mango chutney

Masala dal

Fried ramas slices

Ice-cream

STUFFED MADRASI KOFTA PULAO

• Preparation Time: 20 mins. • Cooking Time: 1 hour • Serves: 10

FOR THE RICE
500 gms. basmati rice
Salt, Ghee

FOR THE GROUND MASALA
1	fresh coconut, milk removed	
1	fresh coconut	
14	reshampatti chillies	Grind
1	whole clove garlic	
3	tbsps. dalia	
3	tbsps. coriander seeds	
1	tbsp. cumin seeds	Broil
1	tbsp. poppy seeds	and
1	tbsp. sesame seeds	grind
1	cup thin tamarind juice made from a lemon sized ball of tamarind.	
20	whole large cashewnuts	

FOR KOFTAS
750	gms. minced mutton
2	onions finely minced
½	cup coriander freshly chopped
¼	cup mint freshly chopped
6	green chillies deseeded and chopped
1"	fresh ginger — ground to a paste
1	sour lime
1	tsp. black pepper ground
8	large slices stale bread
2-3	eggs whisked
6	large tomatoes pulped
½	cup chopped coriander

Salt, Oil, Ghee

Accompaniments:
A Brinjal Salan, A Herb Raita
Chicken Farchas
Sliced Onions, Cucumbers and Lettuce
Custard Apple Basundi

• Broil the spices and grind together with the coconut, reshampatti chillies, garlic and dalia with water to a soft, buttery consistency. Retain the water with which you have washed the grinding stone or mixie. Set aside.

• Mash the mince on the grinding stone to a pulp. Do not wash the mince or the koftas will not hold. Add salt, ground ginger and the finely minced onions, coriander, mint, green chillies, sour lime juice, ground black pepper and mix well in a large thali. Place the bread slices in water and then squeeze the bread between both your hands to remove the water. Add to the mince and mix well. Whisk two eggs and mix into the mince and form a round. Cover and set aside.

• Cook the rice with salt and 1 tablespoon ghee in a rice cooker at the last possible moment after the pulao gravy has been made and the koftas are fried.

• Place a flat bottomed large vessel on the fire with 3 tablespoons of ghee. When the ghee is hot add the ground coconut masala along with salt and fry for 10 minutes on a very low flame. Add the coconut milk, stir and bring to a slow boil. Add tamarind juice. Add the pulped tomatoes and allow to simmer for 10 minutes at least. Remove from the fire.

• Make 15 to 20 portions of the minced mutton according to the size you wish. Flatten each portion in your left hand and place one large cashewnut in the centre and fold the mince into a ball. Fry one in hot oil to see if it holds firm. If it does not, add an extra egg to the mince.

• Deep fry all the koftas to a golden brown and place carefully in the masala gravy.

• Mix the hot rice with the freshly chopped coriander and place in the centre of a dish. Top with the gravy and koftas.

SWEET AND TANGY MINCE AND RIPE MANGO PULAO

• Preparation Time: 15 mins. • Marinating Time: 2-3 hours • Cooking Time: 40 mins. • Serves: 8-10

FOR THE RICE

450 gms. basmati rice
300 gms. onions sliced and fried
1 tbsp. ghee
Salt

FOR THE MANGOES

8 alphonso mangoes cut into 1"
cubes

FOR THE MINCE

2 gms. saffron
800 gms. best quality lamb's meat
made into mince
500 gms. fried and ground onions
300 gms. curd

GROUND MASALA FOR THE MINCE

8 kashmiri chillies
1 cup freshly roasted
cashewnuts
1 tbsp. coarsely ground
fennel seeds
2 tbsps. Prakash's garam
masala

⎫
⎬ Grind
⎮ in a
⎮ little
⎭ water

WHOLE MASALA FOR THE MINCE

1 bunch coriander freshly chopped
6 cloves
2" cinnamon stick
4 bay leaves
Ghee
Salt

FOR THE DECORATION

6 boiled eggs
½ cup black seedless raisins

• Wash the basmati rice and cook with 300 gms. fried onions, 1 large tablespoon ghee and salt in a rice cooker.

• Apply salt to the mince and mix it with the ground onions and ground masala for the mince. Heat the saffron on a griddle. Whip the curd and mix in the saffron and keep for 5 minutes. Then add it to the mince and allow to marinate for 2-3 hours.

• Cut the mangoes, add half a cup of water and cook, covered, over a very low flame for 7 minutes. Keep in a cool place.

• Heat 3 tablespoons ghee in a large vessel and when hot add 6 cloves, 2" cinnamon and 4 bay leaves. Lower the flame to medium and add the mince. Mix vigorously for 10 minutes then allow to cook over a low flame for another 10 minutes. Gradually the gravy will begin to dry up. Add 2 cups of water and cook till tender. If you need more water to cook it add some more without hesitation. The cooked result should be soft but not watery.

• In a high vessel make layers of mangoes, rice and mince and cover tightly and keep on dum for 12 minutes. This pulao is so luscious you can eat it on its own.

Accompaniments:

Gravy fish
Jaggery and Tamarind Hot Chutney
Spring Onion Salad
Tomatoes with Herbs
Firni

MINCE STUFFED TOMATO PULAO

• Preparation Time: 15 mins. • Cooking Time: 50 mins. to 1 hour • Serves: 6

FOR THE RICE

350 gms. basmati rice
2   onions sliced deep fried
4   green cardamoms lightly bruised
4   cloves
10   peppercorns
3   star anise

FOR THE TOMATOES

8   large red tomatoes
300 gms. minced mutton
2   tbsps. coriander freshly cut
1   tbsp. mint freshly cut
1   tbsp. ginger freshly cut
1   tbsp. garlic freshly cut
1   tbsp. green chillies freshly cut
2   onions finely chopped
2   sprig curry leaves
1   tsp. Parsi Dhansakh masala
1   tsp. red kashmiri chilli powder
1   tsp. turmeric powder
1   tsp. garam masala
½   cup sugarcane vinegar   ⎫ Mix
½   cup sugar   ⎬ together
3   bay leaves
½   cup seedless raisins fried
Salt
Pure ghee

• Cook the rice with the fried onions, cardamoms, cloves, peppercorns and star anise in a rice cooker.

• Wash and dry the tomatoes and slice off the tops. Take a small, sharp, pointed knife and with its help as well as that of a small teaspoon collect the seeds and pulp in a small bowl and refrigerate for some other use. Place the tomatoes upside down in a tray so the juice can escape from the emptied tomatoes. Put in a cool place.

• Take the 2 chopped onions and place them in a vessel or large sauce pan. Add 3 tablespoons ghee and cook the onions till soft and pink. Add the ginger and garlic and cook over a low fire for 5 minutes. Then add the coriander, mint, green chillies and curry sprigs and stir for 2 minutes. Add the Parsi Dhansakh masala, garam masala, chilli and turmeric powders and cook for 5 minutes. Turn up the heat, add the mince and salt and stir vigorously up and down and allow to cook in its own juice for 5 minutes. If you like you can add the tomato pulp to the mince along with 1 cup water and cook the mince till soft or you can cook the mince along with 2 cups of water till tender and dry. Taste for salt and tenderness and add more water only if you feel that the mince still has a slightly raw flavour. This will depend on the heat of your stove. Add the vinegar and sugar and cook for 2 more minutes.

• Stuff all the tomatoes with the mince. Take a flat-bottomed vessel. Add 2 tablespoons ghee and the bay leaves. Heat the ghee, lower the flame and place the tomatoes carefully on the base of the vessel. Sprinkle some fine salt. Heat for 5 more minutes, then add 1 cup of water to the pan. If any mince remains add that to the vessel also. Cover with a lid and put some water on the lid and cook the tomatoes till soft but not in a collapsible state. You may need to place more water on the lid as it will evaporate. Also check the water in the vessel and replenish it. Remove from the fire once the tomato shells are cooked.

- Take a large flat dish and place hot pulao rice on it. Make 8 indentations with a spoon and place the 8 tomatoes on them along with any gravy formed in the vessel. Top with the fried raisins and serve immediately.

Accompaniments:

Black Masoor Dal

A Chicken Gravy

Iceberg Lettuce

Sweet Mango Chutney

Badam Halva

STUFFED SNAKE GOURD PULAO

• Preparation Time: 35 mins. • Cooking Time: 1 hour 15 mins. • Serves: 10

This is a delicious and novel item. It takes time to prepare all the ingredients and I would suggest that if possible get a second person to help you to hasten the process of cleaning the gourds, stuffing them, plugging them and frying them. You will have to make two types of rice, so whilst the rice is cooking you must prepare the vegetable for stuffing and the stuffing itself. Clear your kitchen table and arrange stainless steel thalis or trays to keep the cut gourds and the stuffed ones. Remove all the spices for the two rice beforehand and do the same for the stuffing's spices and masalas so that you don't forget anything in your haste. To ensure success you must make sure that the snake gourds are tender and not stringy and old. The type of gourd you use will ensure success or failure of the dish.

FOR THE WHITE RICE

600	gms. basmati rice
3	bay leaves
2	½" pieces cinnamon
4	cloves
4	green cardamoms slightly bruised
1	tbsp. ghee
Salt	

FOR THE CHUTNEY RICE

300	gms. basmati rice	
2	sliced onions deep fried	
½	bunch fresh coriander leaves chopped	
6	green chillies deseeded chopped fine	Grind for the chutney rice
8	large garlic cloves	
1½	tsps. cumin seeds	
2	sour limes	
1½	tsps. sugar	
1½	tsps. ghee	
Salt		

TO PREPARE THE STUFFING

3	snake gourds
750	gms. fresh mutton mince
250	gms. tomatoes finely chopped
250	gms. onions finely chopped
½	cup fresh coriander chopped
2	curry sprigs

• Cook the white rice first along with the bay leaves, cinnamon pieces, cloves, cardamoms and salt in the rice cooker. Once the rice is cooked spread it out to cool in a tray.

• In the same cooker, cook the chutney rice with the ground chutney, fried onions, ghee and salt.

• Whilst both types of rice are cooking prepare the three snake gourds by scraping off the flaky white skin with a sharp knife, or better still get some coarse string made of jute called katha. Make a little bundle of it to fit your palm and scrape the gourd till you get a clear green skin. Cut 3½ inch pieces until you get even-sized 12 pieces from the centre of all three gourds. Clean the pieces of their seeds and soft cottony centres and soak in salted water in a large vessel. Discard the uneven end pieces or make a vegetable dish out of them later.

• Prepare the stuffing by placing the onions and 3 tablespoons pure ghee in a vessel and place over medium heat. When the onion turns pink add the ginger-garlic paste, the mince, the tomatoes and salt and cook stirring all the time for 5 minutes. Lower the flame. Add the curry sprigs, garam masala, turmeric, chilli and clove and cinnamon powders and keep stirring for

1	tbsp. ginger–garlic paste
2	tsps. garam masala
1½	tsps. turmeric powder
1	tsp. chilli powder
1	tsp. clove and cinnamon powder
½	cup sugarcane vinegar ⎤ mix
½	cup melted jaggery ⎦ together
½	cup seedless raisins

Salt
Oil
Ghee

FOR PLUGGING THE GOURD PIECES

Whisked eggs
8   stale bread slices
Salt

FOR DECORATING THE WHITE RICE

100 gms. almonds boiled, skinned,
      sliced, fried
100 gms. pistachios boiled, skinned,
      sliced, fried

5 more minutes. When the mince has fried to a nice red colour add 2 cups of water, mix well and cover. Put water on the cover and allow to cook till tender. If the mince is still raw add some water to it as well as on the cover. Cook till the mince is dry. Mix the jaggery and vinegar and cook over a low flame till the mixture is also absorbed. Set the mince in a tray, sprinkle the fresh coriander and raisins. Taste for salt.

• Drain the snake gourd pieces in a colander.

• Stuff the pieces with the mince and lay in orderly lines in a tray. Stuff them well leaving one quarter inch bare on either side.

• After the stuffing is completed beat 2 eggs in a soup plate. Add half the bread and a pinch of salt and crumble it into the beaten eggs. Add as much bread as the egg mixture can absorb. Then roll the bread and egg mixture into 24 small pellets, circular in nature and stuff each side of the stuffed vegetable pieces with them securely. Allow the bread mixture to set 10 minutes.

• Heat a large karhai ½ full with oil and place over a medium flame. When the oil is hot lower 3 to 4 of the stuffed vegetable pieces gently into it. Pour the hot oil with a long handled spoon over the stuffed vegetable pieces to help them to cook faster. Lower the heat and turn over and when golden brown on both sides remove them onto a large vessel or a tray. Complete frying all the pieces. They should be tender and well cooked.

• If you have a large vessel, you can arrange the pulao in it. If you have 1 or even 2 pyrex high sided dishes they could make the pulao look really beautiful when viewed from the clear glass. If you have neither of these utensils, use 2 small flat bottomed vessels.

- Whatever the vessel or vessels you use, arrange the chutney pulao at the bottom and cover with the stuffed gourd pieces. Then cover with the white rice. If there is any gravy left at the bottom of the vessel pour it over the rice and sprinkle with almond and pistachio slices.

- If using a vessel, place on an iron skillet over medium flame for 15 minutes on dum to allow the aromas to mingle. If using pyrex place in an oven at 325°F for 20 minutes.

Accompaniments:
Vegetable Dhansakh Dal
Onion and Cucumber Kachumber
Makhana ka Raita
Fish Fillets
Rasgoollas floating in Rabri

BHUNE HUA'E MURGH KE KHEEME KA PULAO

• Preparation Time: 10 mins. • Cooking Time: 45 mins. • Serves: 6-8

FOR THE RICE

2	gms. saffron
400	gms. rice ambemohar
200	gms. green peas (raw)
2	onions sliced fried
1	tbsp. coriander seeds coarsely ground
3	cloves
Salt	
Ghee	

FOR THE CHICKEN MINCE

800	gms. chicken made into mince
400	gms. tomatoes skinned chopped
300	gms. onions finely chopped
1	tbsp. ginger-garlic paste
2	spring onions
2	stalks celery finely cut
1	cup fresh coriander finely chopped
¼	cup fresh mint finely chopped
½	cup golden raisins
6	green chillies deseeded
6	red chillies ground in water
2	tbsps. garam masala
1	tsp. turmeric powder
Salt	
Ghee	

DECORATION

100	gms. almonds sliced
10	boiled eggs halved

• Prepare the rice in a rice cooker along with the saffron, green peas, onions, coriander seeds, cloves, salt and ghee.

• Marinate the mince with the salt and ginger-garlic paste. Set aside.

• Place the chopped onions in a vessel. Add 3 tablespoons of ghee and cook over a medium fire till red. Add the mince and mix vigorously and keep stirring up and down so granules don't form. Lower the flame and add all the green and red chillies, the garam masala and turmeric powder. Cook stirring the spices for 5 minutes and then add the tomatoes, spring onions and raisins. Cook over a low fire for 10 more minutes. Then add 1 cup of water at a time till the mince becomes tender. This will take atleast 30 minutes.

• When the mince is tender and only a bare minimum of gravy remains add the celery, fresh coriander and mint and mix well into the mince. Remove from the fire.

• Make two portions of the rice. Take a well-greased vessel and place half the rice on the base. Cover with a layer of mince and then the remaining rice. Spread the almond slices and eggs over the rice and cover well with foil. Place over an iron tava on medium flame for 15 minutes.

Accompaniments:

Fried Liver

Green Salad and Sour Lime Juice

Amla Chutney

Black long Gulabjamuns with

Vanilla ice-cream

KUCCHE-PUKKE AAM AUR MURGHI KE KHEEMA KA PULAO

• Preparation Time: 20 mins. • Cooking Time: 45 mins. • Serves: 8-10

FOR THE RICE

2	gms.	saffron
700	gms.	basmati rice
150	gms.	malai or thick clotted cream
2		star anise
4		green cardamoms crushed
1		litre milk

Salt, 2 tbsps. ghee

MASALA FOR THE CHICKEN MINCE

1200 gms. chicken mince
2 large onions chopped
1 tsp. cumin
1 tbsp. coriander seeds broiled ⎫
½ tbsp. fennel seeds
½ cup fresh coriander chopped
1 tbsp. black pepper ground ⎬ Ground fine
6 green chillies deseeded
1 tbsp. minced ginger
2 tbsps. ambahalad grated ⎭
Salt, Ghee

FOR THE MANGOES

6 alphonso semi-ripe mangoes
1 cup water
½ cup sugar
4 green cardamoms seeds only

FOR THE DECORATION

½ cup pink rose petals
20 almonds sliced, fried
3 drops rose essence.

Accompaniments:

Tomato Raita, Fish Fry Masala
Curd with Cucumber and Cabbage
Fig and Walnut Ice-cream

• Place all the ingredients for rice in the rice cooker. Add water to the milk to make up the liquid quantity necessary to cook the rice. Add salt to taste and cook till tender.

• Peel the mangoes. Cut each cheek into 2 pieces vertically and then cut each piece into 3 horizontally. From the 2 sides of each mango cut 2 pieces. Place the water, sugar and cardamom seeds in a vessel and allow to boil. Add the mango pieces and gently shake the pan till the syrup is absorbed by the fruit. Allow to cool.

• Grind the masala to a fine paste and mix together with the raw mince.

• Chop the onions and cook in 3 tablespoons of ghee till golden in colour. Add the mince and salt and fry non-stop for 7 minutes on a low fire. Add 3 cups of water and bring to a full boil. Reduce heat till mince is soft and tender. In case all your water has evaporated and your mince is still slightly raw, add some more water. When tender, remove from the fire and cool.

• Place the cooked rice in a thali. Mix the rose essence in half a cup of water and sprinkle it on the rice. Sprinkle the rose petals on the rice also.

• Grease a large flat-bottomed vessel on the bottom and sides with ghee. Place half the rice at the base of the vessel. Taste the mince for salt and seasoning and spread it over the rice. Now arrange the mango pieces in a neat layer over the mince using every drop of syrup also and cover with the remaining rice. Sprinkle the sliced onions and almonds over the rice and cover tightly with foil or a lid and dough. Place over an iron griddle on a medium flame for 15 minutes on dum.

PULAO MURGHI ALOO BUKHARI KOFTAS

* Preparation Time: 35 mins. * Cooking Time: 1 hour 25 mins. * Serves: 8-10

FOR THE RICE
500	gms. basmati rice
2	onions sliced fried
4	bay leaves or allspice leaves
2	potatoes skinned and cubed
Salt	
Ghee	

FOR THE ALOO BUKHARI GRAVY
2	onions ground to a pulp	
6	large tomatoes skinned pulped	
10	kashmiri chillies	Grind
1½"	fresh ginger	with
150	gms. broken cashewnuts	a little
1	tbsp. poppy seeds broiled	water
1	tbsp. coriander seeds broiled	
1	tbsp. fennel seeds broiled	
½	tbsp. cumin seeds broiled	
200	gms. cream	
½	cup coriander finely chopped	
½	cup chives cut into 1" pieces	
Salt		
Ghee		

FOR THE ALOO BUKHARI KOFTAS
1500	gms. fresh chicken mince
20	dried apricots soaked overnight in sugar water
1	tbsp. ginger-garlic paste
6	green chillies deseeded and finely chopped
2	tbsps. chopped onions
1	tsp. cumin powder
1	tsp. black pepper powder
1	tsp. cardamom powder
1	tsp. garam masala
4	eggs whisked
Salt	

FOR THE DECORATION
Fried almond slices
4 sheets silver vark

* Cook the rice with all its ingredients and 1 tablespoon ghee in a rice cooker.

* First make the gravy. Take a large vessel and place 1 cup ghee in it and put on a medium flame. When hot, add the pulped onions and fry for 7 minutes until they change colour. Add the ground masala, lower the flame and allow to cook for another 7 minutes. Add the tomatoes, lower the flame even further and allow to simmer for 5 minutes. Add 5 cups of water and simmer for 10 more minutes.

* Place the chicken mince in a thali. Add the salt, ginger-garlic paste, finely chopped green chillies, onions, cumin, black pepper, cardamom and garam masala powders and mix well. Make a hole in the centre of the mince and add the whisked eggs and make a ball and allow to set for 20 minutes.

* Make small flat rounds of mince on the wet palm of your left hand, and place a swollen apricot onto it and seal it in a ball. Fill the rest in the same way. Make the ball tight.

* One by one add the balls to the simmering gravy and cook for 15 minutes. Whip the cream, add to the gravy and remove the vessel from the heat.

* Place the rice on a flat dish and arrange the koftas and gravy on top of it. Sprinkle fried sliced almonds fresh coriander and chives. Apply silver vark to the koftas.

Accompaniments:

Tomato, Lettuce, Onion, Cabbage Salad

Tamarind and Date Chutney

Fish sauce

Shahi Tukra and Chikoo Kulfi

CHICKEN STUFFED ONION PULAO

Preparation Time: 20 mins. • Cooking Time: 1 hour • Serves: 6-8

FOR THE RICE

2	gms. saffron
600	gms. basmati rice
4	crushed green cardamoms
4	bay leaves
3	large onions sliced deep fried
Salt	
Ghee	

FOR THE ONIONS

10	large onions even-sized white or brown
½	cup ground dates
3	sprigs curry leaves
1	cup tamarind pulp
1	cup grated jaggery
1	tsp. red chilli powder
Salt	
Ghee	

FOR THE MINCE

500	gms. fine chicken mince
300	gms. thick curd
200	gms. tomatoes skinned, finely chopped
1½	tbsp. ginger-garlic paste
Salt	
Ghee	

FOR THE MINCE MASALA

1"	cinnamon	
3	mace flowers	
½	tsp. shahjeera seeds	
4	cloves	Grind
1	tsp. broken star anise	very
15	black peppercorns	fine
8–10	long light green chillies deseeded. (Not the dark green pungent ones.)	with a little water
1	cup coriander finely chopped	
¼	cup mint finely chopped	

• Divide the rice into 2 portions and cook one with half the fried onions and all the whole spices in a rice cooker. Cook the other half with saffron, remaining fried onions, salt and ghee.

• Take the onions, skin them and cut off the tops. Using a very sharp knife or teaspoon, scoop out the insides carefully. The outer skin should not be cut at all. Hollow out the insides leaving a strong circular shell. Salt the onions inside and outside and set aside.

• Take a vessel and add 1½ tablespoons ghee and place over medium flame. Add the ginger-garlic paste, mince and salt and mix vigorously for 5 minutes. Lower the flame and allow to cook for another 5 minutes. Add the tomatoes and allow to simmer for 10 minutes. Add the ground masala and mix well. Also add 1 cup of water obtained after washing the grinding stone or mixie. Cover and allow to simmer. Taste for salt. Cook till the mince is tender and dry and then add the curd and allow the mince to dry up.

• Stuff the mince into the salted onions until it overflows. Place a flat-bottomed vessel with 2 tablespoons of ghee in it over a very low flame. Allow the ghee to get hot and carefully place all the onions in a single layer at the bottom of the vessel. Add the curry leaves and a cup of water and cover and cook over a low flame for 10 minutes.

• Meanwhile place the tamarind pulp, grated jaggery, ground dates, 1 teaspoon chilli powder and salt in a large saucepan and bring to a boil. Add 1 cup of water and boil for 10 minutes. Slowly pour this sauce into the vessel holding the

FOR THE DECORATION

4 boiled eggs quartered
½ cup raisins fried
½ cup almonds flaked fried

stuffed onions, from one side. Cover and cook till the onions are tender.

- Place the rice with the whole spice at the bottom of a very large vessel. Spread the rice, level it and make ten holes in it and place each onion into a hollow. With a ladle pour the gravy around the onions and carefully cover with the saffron rice. The tops of the onions should show. If any mince is left over pour it over the rice. Cover with an airtight lid and dough. Place the vessel on a tava over medium heat for 25 minutes. Open and serve on a silver salver, decorated with the quartered eggs, fried raisins and fried almonds.

Accompaniments:

Fried Fish Fillets
Russian Salad
Hot Mango and Raisin chutney
Baked Apple Pudding

TAMATERON KE DULME KA ZAFFRANI PULAO

• Preparation Time: 25 mins. • Cooking Time: 1 hour • Serves: 8-10

FOR THE RICE

2	gms. saffron
700	gms. basmati rice
3	onions, sliced
5	bay leaves
4	green cardamoms crushed
½	tsp. nigella seeds
½	tsp. fennel seeds
Salt	
Ghee	

FOR THE GRAVY

½	fresh coconut grated	
12	reshampatti chillies deseeded	
1	cup broken cashewnuts	
½	grated beetroot	Ground to a fine paste
2	grated onions	
1	sour lime sized tamarind ball	
1	tbsp. broiled coriander seeds	
1	tsp. sesame seeds	
Salt		
Ghee		

FOR THE STUFFED TOMATOES

12	tomatoes large and even-sized
800	gms. chicken mince
1	cup tomato ketchup
2	large onions finely chopped
6	green chillies deseeded and finely chopped
2	tsps. cinnamon, cloves and black pepper powdered
1	tbsp. ginger and garlic paste
½	cup coriander freshly chopped
Salt	
Ghee	

• Place the onions alongwith 2 tablespoons of ghee in a vessel and add the whole spices when the onion becomes soft and golden in colour. Fry for 3 minutes and add the washed rice and fry for 5 minutes. Empty the rice into a rice cooker alongwith salt. Heat the saffron and crumble it directly upon the rice. Add sufficient water to cook rice till tender. Empty the rice on a large thali to cool.

• First wash and dry the tomatoes. Take a sharp, thin knife and cut the top of each tomato. With a tiny teaspoon, which is sharp edged, collect the seeds and pulp into a bowl. Refrigerate and use it in some other dish. Place the tomatoes upside down on a rack so that juice from the tomatoes can drain away. After 15 minutes salt them lightly from the inside and place them upside down again on the rack.

• Grind the gravy masala until it is soft and buttery. Reserve the water with which you have washed the grinding stone or mixie.

• Place 2 tablespoons ghee in a large frying pan. When hot, add the masala and fry it well non-stop till red. Cook for 5 minutes after which add the water from the washed mixie or grinding stone. Lower the flame and add salt and allow to cook for 10 minutes till the gravy bubbles and boils. Remove from the stove and cool. Taste for salt.

• Place the finely chopped onions in a large saucepan alongwith 2 tablespoons of ghee and cook till soft. Add the chicken mince, the ginger-garlic paste and salt and turn up and down for 7 minutes. Gradually add the chopped coriander, green chillies, powdered spices, and the ketchup. Allow the mince to cook in its own juice for 10 minutes on a very low fire. Then add 2 cups of water, cover with a lid and place water on it and allow the mince to cook till dry. If the mince is not tender, add more water and cook till it dries up. Stuff each of the tomatoes with mince, after tasting for salt.

* Take a large flat-bottomed vessel. Grease the base lavishly with ghee and arrange the tomatoes on it. Add 2 cups of water, cover and place water on the cover and cook the tomato shells till soft.

* Place all the rice in a greased tray. Make 12 depressions in the rice and place the stuffed tomatoes in them. Top the rice and the tomatoes with the gravy and bake for 15 minutes at 350°F. If you don't have an oven don't worry. Heat some coals on a wire mesh on your gas stove. Cover the tray and place some live coals on the cover and heat the tray over a very, very low flame.

* Serve the stuffed tomato pulao from the tray itself. By transferring it to a glass dish it will spoil its appearance as well as get cold faster.

Accompaniments:
Prawn Patia
A Hot Salad of Rajma
Vegetable Curry
Mango Shrikhand

FRENY'S MINCE-STUFFED BRINJAL PULAO

• Preparation Time: 20 mins. • Cooking Time: 40 mins. • Serves: 4-6

FOR THE RICE

450	gms. basmati rice
2	onions chopped fine and deep fried
3	green cardamom seeds
½	tsp. broiled coriander seeds
½	tsp. broiled cumin seeds
10	black peppercorns
½	large red bell pepper minced
1½	tbsps. pure ghee
Salt	

FOR THE BRINJALS

4	large round pink brinjals or any other kind
1	tsp. oil
Juice of 1 sour lemon	
Salt	

FOR THE STUFFING

750	gms. mutton mince
1	large onion finely chopped
4	large tomatoes skinned and finely chopped
1	tbsp. crushed ambahalad
½	cup chives chopped into ½" pieces
½	cup red carrots grated
½	cup raisins soaked overnight in water
½	cup sugarcane vinegar
½	cup brown sugar
1½	tsps. chilli powder
1½	tsps. garam masala
1	pinch mace
Ghee or refined oil	
Salt	

FOR THE DECORATION

8	mint sprigs

• Mix the mince, ambahalad and salt and set aside while you peel and chop the onions. Place the chopped onions in a large pan, add 2 tablespoons of ghee and heat over a low flame. When pink add the mince, lower the flame still further, and cook for 5 minutes, stirring non-stop. Add the grated carrots, tomatoes and powdered spices and stir for 3 minutes. Add 3 cups of water, cover partly and cook till soft. When tender, add the sugar and vinegar and dry up the mince. Finally add the raisins, stir and set aside. Taste for salt.

• Wash the rice and place in an electric cooker. Add the fried onions, coarsely ground masalas, whole black peppercorns, minced red pepper, ghee and salt and cook till fluffy.

• See the picture and then cut the brinjals evenly from the top of the stem till you get 2 equal portions. Scoop out the soft portion and leave a thin shell like a cup. Stuff them with the mince. Oil the brinjals from outside and place them in an oven at 350°F. Add 1 cup of water. Cover each brinjal with foil and allow to cook till soft.

• Place the cooked rice in a stainless steel tray or an oval pyrex dish. Cover with the hot brinjals.

Accompaniments:

Banana Raita

Mango Chhunda

Fried Chillies

Palak and Paneer

Rasagoollas

A BOMBAY DUCK SURPRISE

• Preparation Time: 25 mins. • Cooking Time: 50 mins. • Serves: 6-8

FOR THE RICE

400	gms. basmati rice
5	spring onions from base to 6" upward cut fine julienne
10	peppercorns
1	tsp. broiled cumin
1	tsp. fennel seeds broiled
4	cloves
½	tsp. yellow pulao colour

Pure ghee, Salt

FOR THE FISH AND BATTER

20	Bombay ducks of medium size scaled, heads and 1" above the tails cut off. Washed in rice or gram flour, then plain water, salted and set aside.
1	cup gram flour
1	cup thick tamarind water
1	large onion minced finely
2	tbsps. coriander finely chopped
1	tbsp. green chillies (long ones) deseeded and finely chopped
1	tbsp. mint finely chopped
1½	tsps. chilli powder
1	tsp. turmeric powder
½	tsp. sambar powder
1	tsp. garlic pulp

Bread crumbs, Salt, Oil

FOR THE FISH GRAVY

14	green chillies deseeded
1	tbsp. black mustard seeds
1	large pod garlic
1½	tbsps. cumin seeds
10	black peppercorns
2	cups chopped coriander
½	cup mint leaves lightly packed
½	cup grated coconut
½	cup sugarcane vinegar

Grind in a little Vinegar

• Cook the rice along with the spring onions, peppercorns, cumin, fennel and cloves, yellow colour, salt and 1 tablespoon ghee. Cook in an electric cooker and spread out on a thali to cool.

• Fillet and salt the fish and prepare the batter by placing the gram flour and tamarind water in a large bowl and mixing it together. Add all the other ingredients such as chopped onions, coriander, chillies, mint, chilli powder, turmeric powder, sambar powder, garlic pulp and salt. Gradually add a trickle of water so that the thick mixture becomes liquidy enough to coat the fillets. Taste for salt.

• Place a flat non-stick frying pan half filled with oil on medium heat. When the oil is hot, dip the fish fillets in breadcrumbs and then in batter and fry crisp in batches, till golden brown. Keep aside.

• Take a vessel and put in 3 tablespoons of the leftover oil. Add the curry sprigs and when they crackle add the ground masala and fry till it emits a delicious aroma. Lower the flame, add salt and 2 cups of water and cook till you get a thick gravy. Taste for salt.

• Divide the rice into 2 portions and put 1 portion of the rice at the bottom of a greased vessel. Pour the gravy over the rice and arrange the fillets neatly in a layer on top. Cover with the rest of the rice and then sprinkle the fried onions on top.

• Place over an iron griddle on medium heat for 15 minutes.

Accompaniments:

Coconut curry

Rice Papads

Chilli kachumber with lime juice and onions

Banana Raita

Ananas-ka-muzaffar

MAPLAH MEEN (FISH) BIRYANI

• Preparation Time: 15 mins. • Cooking Time: 1 hour 10 mins. • Serves: 8-10

FOR THE RICE

800	gms. basmati rice
2	(2") pieces cinnamon
4	corns allspice
4	black peppercorns
3	medium onions sliced and deep fried

Salt
Ghee

FOR THE FISH

1500	gms. fillets of Bekti, Surmai, Ramas or Pomfrets
500	gms. onions finely chopped
750	gms. tomatoes skinned chopped
1	bunch fresh coriander chopped
½	bunch fresh mint chopped
1	cup thick tamarind juice
2	tbsps. fresh ginger coarsely crushed
1	whole large pod garlic crushed
6	spring onions uptil 6" cut julienne from root, cut julienne
6	green chillies deseeded and chopped
4	sprigs curry leaves

Salt
Coconut oil

FOR THE GROUND MASALA

2"	fresh turmeric	
10	red reshampatti chillies	
1	tbsp. coriander seeds	Grind in a little water
½	tbsp. anise (saunf)	
8	green chillies deseeded	
1	tbsp. garam masala	

FOR THE DECORATION

2	onions sliced and deep fried crisply
1	cup broken cashew nuts fried
¾	cup raisins fried

• Place the fried onions, cinnamon, allspice and peppercorns into a vessel. Add 1½ tablespoon ghee and fry over medium heat for 3 minutes. Add rice, washed twice and fry for 5 minutes. Add salt and cook in the rice cooker.

• Wash and salt the fish fillets. Apply the chilli-turmeric paste and sprinkle with 2 tablespoons of tamarind juice and set aside.

• Place the chopped onions in a large vessel with 1 cup coconut oil and cook till soft. Add the curry leaves, ginger, garlic and fry along with the onions for 5 minutes. Add the second ground masala, lower the flame and cook for 5 minutes. Then add the chopped tomatoes and the green chillies, cut coriander and mint and cook to a thick paste. Taste for salt. Add the tamarind juice. Cook for 5 more minutes.

• Place coconut oil in a frying pan over medium heat and when hot lower the flame and fry the fish fillets till golden brown. Add them to the cooked onion and tomato mixture and turn the fish upside down so that it is smothered in the masala sauce.

• Place the cooked rice in a thali and mix in the fried onions, cashewnuts and raisins.

• Take a large biryani vessel and grease the bottom and sides with ghee. Spread a layer of rice and sprinkle a little of the spring onions on top. Then spread a layer of fish. Repeat till all the rice and fish is used. Sprinkle the topmost layer of rice with half a cup of water. Cover with a tight fitting lid and dough. Place on an iron tava over medium heat for 30 minutes. Allow to rest for 10 minutes and serve very hot with papads and pickles.

Accompaniments:

Mutter paneer, Coriander and Mint Chutney
Plain Curd, Almond Kheer

MACCHI NO PULAO — FISH PULAO

FOR THE RICE

1	gm. saffron
400	gms. basmati rice
3	sliced onions deep fried golden
1	dry red chilli broken into 3 parts
10	black peppercorns
2	(1") pieces cinnamon
4	cloves

FOR THE FISH

800	gms. thick fish fillets of ramas or ghol fish

FOR THE MASALA

12	kashmiri chillies	
1	whole clove garlic	
1½	tbsps. cumin	
½	tsp. whole black mustard seeds	Grind with water
6	black peppercorns	
1	knob tamarind	
3	bunches spring onions	
4	large tomatoes	
½	cup finely chopped coriander	
2	raw mangoes cut into chips	
3	sprigs curry leaves	

Salt
Mustard oil
Ghee

• Prepare the rice with the saffron, sliced fried onions, red chilli bits, black peppercorns, cloves and 1 tablespoon ghee. Once cooked spread out on a thali to cool.

• Wash the fish twice and add salt to taste. Grind the masala till soft. Retain the water with which you wash the grinding stone or mixie.

• Place 2 or 3 tablespoons of mustard oil in a vessel. Place on a medium flame. Add the curry sprigs, cook for 2 minutes and add the ground masala and fry for 5 minutes till red. Add the water from the grinding stone. It should be atleast 2 cups. Bring to a boil and gently add the fish fillets. Hold the vessel with a kitchen cloth in both your hands and sway the vessel to and fro so that the masala does not stick to the bottom of the pan and the fish gets covered by the masala. Add the mango chips and lower the heat and cook gently for 10 minutes.

• Place half the hot rice on a salver. Cover with the fish fillets and masala gravy with the mango chips. Cover with the remaining rice. Serve hot.

Accompaniments:

Green salad

Lime pickles and papads

Cooked spinach

Hot jalebis in syrup

"MURI GHANTO" PULAO
(Nilanjana Roy's Bengali dish called "Fish Head" Pulao served to the Jamai or Bridegroom)

• Preparation Time: 10 mins. • Cooking Time: 45-50 mins. • Serves: 4-6

600	gms. basmati rice
2	large fish heads of ruhi, bekti, ramas or ghol
4	onions sliced and deep fried to golden brown
15	small potatoes boiled in their jackets
4	cloves
2"	cinnamon
4	cardamoms crushed
10	black peppercorns
1½	tbsps. turmeric paste
2	tbsps. kashmiri chilli paste
12	large garlic cloves made into paste
2	tbsps. sugar

Mustard oil or peanut oil for frying
Salt
Pure ghee

• Wash the rice and place it aside. Cut the fish heads into large pieces. Wash twice, salt them and set aside.

• Place a ¼ of the fried onions into a pan and add the whole spices, cloves, cinnamon, cardamom and black peppercorns along with 2 tablespoons of pure ghee. Add 2 tablespoons of water and cook over a low fire till a nice aroma is emitted. Add the sugar and stir. Add sufficient water to the rice and salt and cover and cook on medium heat till the rice is almost done or cook in an electric rice cooker.

• Whilst the rice is cooking, apply the turmeric, chilli and garlic paste on the fish. After 30 minutes, deep-fry the fish pieces in hot mustard oil in 2 or 3 batches and place above the almost cooked rice and cover so that it absorbs the essence of the rice and vice versa. Fry the baby potatoes after peeling and salting them and add to the rice. Cover the lid tightly and allow to settle for 10 minutes.

• Decorate with mint spears and sour lime wedges after sprinkling the rice with the remaining crisply fried onions.

Accompaniments:
Spicy Tomato Chutney
Sautéed Boiled Eggs with Vegetables
Kesri Rava loaded with Golden Raisins

BENGALI FISH PULAO

· Preparation Time: 15 mins. · Cooking Time: 50 mins. · Serves: 6-8

This is a somewhat unusual way of cooking the rice and reminds one of the way it is cooked in northern India in the mutton yakhni itself. The fragrance of the pulao is very delicious in an airy, light way. The fish taste does not detract from the delicate fragrance of the rice.

FOR THE RICE

600	gms. basmati rice
2	large onions coarsely chopped
1	tbsp. broiled coriander seeds crushed
1	tbsp. broiled anise seeds crushed
1	tbsp. broiled cumin seeds crushed
4	green cardamoms crushed
3	flowers mace crushed
1½"	piece chopped ginger
1	tbsp. pure ghee
Salt	

FOR THE FISH

10	(2½") fillets of rahu, mahseer, ghol or pomfret fish
3	sprigs curry leaves
15	large garlic cloves finely sliced
Mustard oil	

FOR THE GROUND MASALA

6	kashmiri chillies
1	cup finely chopped fresh coriander
2	tbsps. freshly chopped mint
1	tbsp. anise seeds
1	tbsp. turmeric powder
½	tbsp. cumin seeds broiled
2	sour limes for their juice

Grind with half a cup of water

FOR THE DECORATION

2	sliced onions deep fried and crisp

· Wash the rice and keep it aside. Place a large pot on a medium flame with sufficient water to cook your rice in an electric rice cooker. Add 2 cups extra for evaporation whilst boiling. Take all the crushed spices, the raw onion and ginger and tie it all up in a large square muslin cloth. Tie the four ends together with a long white cord, which should extend from the pot to the table so that you can pull it up easily. Boil the water for 25 minutes at a fast boil. Put the washed rice in the rice cooker, add salt and the necessary amount of water. Cook till fluffy and tender.

· Grind all the masala, till soft. Squeeze the lime juice in it and spread the masala all over the salted fish fillets.

· Place 3 tablespoons of mustard oil in a frying pan over moderate heat. Allow the oil to smoke, then reduce the heat and add the curry leaves and the sliced garlic. Stir for 2 minutes and fry the fish till crisp in 2 or 3 batches. Place it in a thali.

· Remove the hot rice onto a salver and dot with pure ghee and place the fried fish pieces on top of the rice. Cover with the crisp fried onions.

Accompaniments:

A green salad and sour lime wedges
Spicy egg curry
Chum-chum

PARSI MACCHI-NE-TAMBOTA NO PULAO

• Preparation Time: 20 mins. • Cooking Time: 50 mins. • Serves: 6-8

FOR THE RICE

400	gms. basmati rice
3	bay leaves
1	tbsp. ghee
Salt	

FOR THE FISH GRAVY

12	thick white fish fillets: pomfret or ramas or ghol or bekti or surmai
2	onions finely chopped
900	gms. large red tomatoes skinned and deseeded
1	cup ladyfingers finely chopped
1	cup coriander finely chopped
2	tbsps. sugar
1	tsp. oregano
Refined sunflower oil	
Salt	

FOR THE GROUND MASALA

8	green chillies deseeded
1	large pod garlic
2	tbsps. cumin broiled
2	tbsps. coriander seeds broiled
2	tsps. red chilli powder

Grind in a little water

FOR THE DECORATION

4	boiled eggs shelled and quartered
2	onions sliced and deep fried

• Cook the rice along with the bay leaves, salt and ghee in a rice cooker.

• Grind the masala till fine and reserve the water with which you wash your grinding stone or mixie.

• Deep fry the ladyfingers, sprinkle fine salt on them and set aside.

• Pulp the tomatoes with the help of 1 cup of water.

• Place 1 cup of ghee in a non-stick frying pan. Salt the fillets and deep fry them in small batches. Empty any left-over ghee onto the cooked rice.

• Put some refined sunflower oil in a large vessel and place over medium flame. Add the chopped onions and cook till pink and soft. Add the ground masala, lower the flame and stir the masala well for 5 minutes. Add the oregano, stir, add tomato pulp, sugar and allow to simmer for 10 minutes.

• Drop the fillets in the simmering tomato gravy, one by one and cook for 5 minutes. Sprinkle the chopped coriander.

• Place the rice in a large rectangular, pyrex or aluminium dish. Cover with the fish in neat lines. Top with the gravy. Arrange the boiled egg quarters on top of the fish along with the deepfried ladyfingers and onions. Bake in an oven at 350°F for 20 minutes. Serve.

Accompaniments:

Corn and Capsicum Salad

Vegetable Cutlets

Raisin and Ginger Chutney

Gulabjamuns with Ice-cream

PARSI NARGOLIO PRAWN PULAO

FOR THE RICE

500	gms. basmati rice
3	onions sliced deep fried
10	allspice corns lightly crushed
Salt	
Ghee	

FOR THE PRAWNS

45	large prawns shelled and deveined
4	large onions chopped
6	large tomatoes skinned and pulped
3	coarse thick lemon grass stalks
¼	cup chopped coriander
3	sprigs curry leaves
Salt	
Peanut oil	

FOR THE GROUND MASALA

7	green chillies deseeded	
8	kashmiri chillies deseeded and broiled	
16	black peppercorns	Grind fine in half a cup of water
1	tbsp. coriander seeds broiled	
1	tsp. cumin seeds broiled	
1	tsp. fennel seeds broiled	
1"	fresh turmeric	
1"	fresh ginger	
1	whole pod garlic	

• Cook the rice along with the fried onions, allspice corns, salt and 1 tablespoon of ghee in a rice cooker.

• Wash and salt the prawns and set aside.

• Grind the masala very fine. Reserve the water with which you wash your grinding stone or mixie.

• Place the chopped onions in a vessel with 2 tablespoons of peanut oil and the lemon grass leaves and place over medium heat. Cook till pink and soft and add the curry sprigs. Fry for 2 minutes and add the ground masala and the prawns. Lower the flame and cook for 5 minutes. Add 1 cup of water and cover and cook for another 7 minutes. Add the tomato pulp and cook till you get a strong, thick paste and the prawns are tender. Taste for salt and remove from the flame. Remove the lemon grass leaves.

• Place the hot rice straight from the cooker onto a platter and scatter the prawn mixture over it. Top with the chopped fresh coriander and serve at once.

Accompaniments:

Fried Dried Fish

A thin dal

Green Salad with cucumber in lime sauce

Gulabjamuns or Fried Parsi Sev with sweetened cream

TIGER PRAWN BIRYANI

• Preparation Time: 30 mins. • Marinate overnight • Cooking Time: 40 mins. • Serves: 4-6

Tiger prawns are very expensive and are considered a luxury item. You must see that they are very fresh when you buy them. When you reach home, immediately plunge them in ice water. First of all remove all the thick, strong legs, which are attached to the prawn's belly and mouth. Then do not shell them. Hold each one by the tail and cut it off below the eyes. Skin them carefully by leaving the skin on the tails. Then devein them with a small sharp knife and gently wash twice, each time in clean, clear water. Marinate them in sour lime juice and salt, overnight, in a refrigerator for best results.

FOR THE RICE

400	gms. basmati rice
4	bay leaves
½	tsp. carraway seeds
70%	tomato juice pure
30%	water
½	cup tomato ketchup
Salt, Ghee	

FOR THE TIGER PRAWNS

24	large fresh tiger prawns
4	sour limes for juice
2	large onions chopped
20	baby onions
½	cup parsley
300	gms. tomatoes skinned, deseeded, pulped
½	cup coriander freshly chopped
Salt, Ghee	

• Cook the rice along with the bay leaves, carraway seeds, 70% tomato juice, 30% water, ½ cup tomato ketchup, salt and 1½ tablespoons of ghee in a rice cooker. Use tomato juice and water carefully as the rice should not be sticky.

• Grind the masala very fine and apply it to the prawns marinated in limejuice and salt overnight. Allow to reach room temperature.

• Place the chopped onions in a large vessel with 1½ cups ghee and place over a medium flame. Allow to cook till soft. Add the tiger prawns and the ground masala, lower the flame, cover the vessel, and allow to cook gently in their own juice for 7 minutes.

1. *Freny's Mince-stuffed Brinjal Pulao*
2. *Mango chhunda*
3. *Palak Paneer*
4. *Rasagoollas*

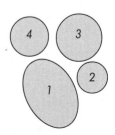

GROUND MASALA FOR THE PRAWNS

6	kashmiri dried chillies deseeded	
4	fresh green chillies deseeded	Grind together in the tamarind pulp
10	black peppercorns	
1"	piece fresh ginger	
10	cloves garlic	
1	tsp. broiled cumin	
1	star anise	
½	cup tamarind pulp	

GROUND CASHEWNUTS FOR THE TIGER PRAWNS

150 gms. broken cashewnuts ground in ½ to 1 cup water

FOR THE DECORATION

½ cup chive pieces 1" long
½ cup fried peanuts
½ cup red pomegranate seeds

- Uncover the vessel and add in the baby onions, the parsley and the chopped tomatoes. Stir gently over a very low flame and allow to simmer for 10 minutes. Taste for salt. If you feel it is necessary add 1 cup of water and cook till the prawns are soft and tender. Add the ground cashewnuts along with the water used for washing your grinding stone or mixie and cook for a further 10 minutes. Remove from the fire. Spread the cooked rice over the tiger prawns, cover with a lid and dough and place on an iron tava for 25 minutes over a medium flame.

- Remove onto a silver platter and arrange the tiger prawns in a circle over the rice. Decorate with the chopped chives, fried pinenuts and pomegranate seeds.

Accompaniments:

Hyderabadi Khatte Baingan
Dahi Vadas
Pineapple Orange Salad
Tandoori Murghi
Chocolate Mousse

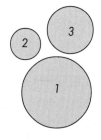

1. Saraswat Brahmin Prawn Pulao
2. Coriander Coconut Chutney
3. Brinjal Capsicum Salan

SARASWAT BRAHMIN PRAWN PULAO

- Preparation Time: 20 mins. • Cooking Time: 50 mins. • Serves: 6-8

The Saraswats are to be found in Goa, Karwar, Ratnagiri and Vengurla in the Konkan as well as South Kanara. This is an unusual recipe of theirs.

FOR THE RICE

700	gms. long grained rice	
4	cardamoms seeds only	
1"	cinnamon	Grind finely
6	black peppercorns	
1	tbsp. poppy (khus khus) seeds	
3	mace flowers	

1	onion	Grind to a paste
½	small coconut	

Salt
Ghee

FOR THE PRAWNS

1	kg. prawns	
½	small coconut for extracting milk	
4	deseeded green chillies	Grind to a fine paste with a little water
1	small pod garlic	
2	(1") pieces ginger	
1	cup fresh coriander chopped	
1	tsp. turmeric	
3	large onions finely chopped	
1	large onion sliced	
2	sprigs curry leaves	
½	cup tamarind pulp	

Salt
Coconut or any other oil

Accompaniments:

A salad of raw onions, beetroots and cucumber

A brinjal-capsicum salan

Sweet curd with apples

Rice kheer with nuts

- Grind the masalas very fine. Retain water from the grinding stone and/or mixie.

- Wash the prawns twice after deveining them. Salt them.

- Grind one onion with half a grated coconut and set aside.

- Chop three onions finely and place in a vessel with the curry sprigs and with ¾ cup of oil. Cook till the onion turns pink and soft. Lower the flame and add the ginger–garlic-chilli-coriander paste and cook for 3 minutes. Add the prawns and the water from the grinding stone and cover and cook till tender. Add the turmeric and the tamarind pulp and cook for a further 7 minutes. Taste for salt. Remove from the fire.

- Add 1 tablespoon of ghee to a frying pan and fry the spices — cardamom seeds, cinnamon, black peppercorns, poppy seeds and mace flowers and grind them to a paste. Extract milk from the remaining half coconut.

- Wash rice twice and apply the spice paste to it.

- Heat the oil in a karhai and deep fry the sliced onion till golden brown and crisp. Place the onion in a vessel and add the raw rice with the masala paste to it. Add 1 tablespoon of the oil in which the onion had been fried and fry the rice in it for 5 minutes. Add the onion-coconut paste and cook for 5 minutes more.

- Place the rice in a rice cooker. Add salt. Take the coconut milk and measure it. Add sufficient water to it to cook the rice fluffy and tender.

- Mix the hot rice with the cooked prawns and serve immediately.

KERALA PRAWN BIRYANI

FOR THE RICE

600	gms. basmati rice
4	bay leaves
2"	piece cinnamon broken into 3
10	peppercorns
2	onions sliced deep fried
1½	tbsps. pure ghee
Salt	

FOR THE PRAWNS

1	kg. large prawns
3	onions sliced
1	cup fresh coriander finely cut
½	cup mint finely chopped
Juice of 2 sour limes	
250	gms. curd
6	green chillies split deseeded
6	green cardamoms crushed
6	cloves
2	(1") pieces cinnamon
10	cracked black peppercorns
3	sprigs curry leaves
Salt	
Ghee	

FOR THE GROUND MASALA

½	freshly grated coconut
8	red dried reshampatti chillies
1	large pod garlic
1½"	piece fresh ginger sliced
1½	tsps. aniseeds

} Grind in a little water

- Shell, devein and wash the prawns and marinate them in salt and half the sour lime juice.

- Cook the rice along with the bay leaves, cinnamon, peppercorns, fried onions, half the lime juice, salt and ghee in a rice cooker.

- Place a vessel over a medium fire. Add 1 cup of ghee and deep-fry the sliced onions till golden. Then whilst the onions are cooking add in the whole spices and curry leaves. Add the ground masala and lower the flame and cook till well fried and red. Do not allow it to stick to the pan. Add the prawns and mix well and cook over a low heat. Add the split green chillies and taste for salt. When the ghee starts separating and prawns are tender, taste for salt. Add curd and set aside.

- Take a large vessel, grease it with oil on the inside and spread half the rice at the bottom. Cover with the cooked prawns and all its thick gravy and cover it with the rest of the rice. Place a tight lid on the vessel and apply dough. Place on a slow fire and put coals on the lid and cook for 20 minutes. Serve hot covered with the chopped coriander and mint.

Accompaniments:

Beetroot Raita

Pineapple Chutney with Fried Chicken

Cauliflower in Coconut Gravy

Sago Pudding

JUMBO PRAWN FANTASY PULAO

• Preparation Time: 20 mins. • Cooking Time: 40 mins. • Serves: 6

FOR THE RICE

400	gms. basmati rice
750	gms. red tomatoes pulped
1	tbsp. broiled cumin coarsely ground
1	cup tomato ketchup
2	onions sliced and fried
1	tbsp. ghee
Salt	

FOR THE JUMBO PRAWNS

20	large jumbo prawns. Keep the shell of the tail intact. Cut the head off near the eyes, remove the long claws and devein and wash thrice.
4	spring onions
400	gms. mushrooms sliced
3	sour limes for juice
10	sweet, long, fat chillies intact
1	tbsp. black peppercorns freshly ground
2	tbsps. sugar
Salt	
Ghee	

FOR THE GROUND MASALA

10	reshampatti red chillies
1½"	piece fresh ginger
10	cloves garlic
½	tsp. mustard seeds

One pinch each:
Cinnamon and mace powders
2" ambahalad

Grind together with a little sugarcane vinegar

• Wash the prawns well. Marinate in the sour lime juice, black pepper powder and salt. Set aside.

• Grind the masala till soft. Remove the water from the grinding stone or mixie for use.

• Heat 50 gms. ghee in a vessel, add the fried onions and washed rice and mix with salt and stir for 5 minutes. Add the pulped tomatoes and the ketchup and cook in the rice cooker. Add only as much tomato pulp as necessary. Taste for salt.

• Heat 75-100 gms. ghee in a heavy based, flat vessel. Add the masala and stir for 7 minutes till it is cooked and emits a wonderful aroma. Lower the flame and add the jumbo prawns. Turn carefully so that the heads do not separate. Taste the masala for salt. Cover tightly and cook till tender in the prawn juice. Open after 12 minutes and stir. Check for tenderness and salt. Only if it is necessary add ½ cup to 1 cup water to tenderize the prawns.

• When the prawns are cooked, wash and cut the spring onions diagonally.

• Spread the rice on a salver and arrange the jumbo prawns and the thick gravy on it. Decorate with the spring onions and the sweet chillies. If you like you can cook them for 1 minute in hot ghee. Serve this rice on its own. It does not need an accompaniment.

A PULAO OF BABY BRINJALS STUFFED WITH SHRIMPS

• Preparation Time: 25 mins. • Cooking Time: 1 hour • Serves: 6-8

FOR THE RICE

1½	tsps. yellow pulao colour
450	gms. basmati rice
3	onions sliced and deep fried
3	bay leaves
1	tsp. nigella seeds
1	tsp. coriander seeds
½	cup green peas
1	tbsp. ghee
Salt	

FOR THE BRINJALS

15	baby brinjals washed and cut into 4 upto ¾ way
2	cups baby pink shrimps washed thrice
6	green chillies deseeded ⎫ Ground in a
6	large garlic cloves ⎭ little water
1½	tsps. cumin
Thin white string	
3	tbsps. sugarcane vinegar
3	tbsps. jaggery
1	tsp. turmeric powder
2	tsps. parsi dhansakh masala
Salt, Peanut oil	

FOR THE GRAVY

2	onions finely chopped
Thick milk from ½ coconut	
400	gms. tomatoes skinned deseeded pulped
1	tsp. chilli powder
1½	tsps. garam masala
2	sprigs curry leaves
Salt, Ghee	

Accompaniments:

Vegetable Curry

Red Cabbage Salad with Curd

Tandoori Chicken

Paruppu Payasam

• Cook the rice in a pan alongwith the washed green peas, fried onions, bay leaves, nigella and coriander seeds in the ghee. Stir well for 5 minutes and add the salt, water and the yellow colour and then put everything in the rice cooker. When cooked, spread on a thali to cool.

• Make the gravy by cooking the chopped onions and curry leaves in 2 tablespoons ghee till onions are pink and soft. Then add the pulped tomatoes and allow to form a thick paste. Add the thick coconut milk and allow to simmer over a low flame for 10 minutes. Add the chilli, garam masala powders, salt and cook for a further 5 minutes. Remove from the fire.

• Place the cut baby brinjals in a large pan of salted water. Wash the shrimps thrice and salt them.

• Place 2 tablespoons of oil in a large frying pan over a medium flame. When hot add the ground masala and mix for 5 minutes. Add the salted baby shrimps, turmeric and dhansakh powders and allow to cook on a low flame till the shrimps are cooked.

• Stuff the brinjals to bursting point with the shrimps and tie them with the string so that the shrimps don't fall out. Grate the jaggery in a clean flat bottomed vessel and add the vinegar and 1 cup of water with a pinch of salt. Place the brinjals in the melted liquid and cover and cook over a low flame till the brinjals are soft but not mushy.

• Divide the rice into 2 portions. Place half the rice at the bottom of a large vessel. Spread the gravy on top of the rice and arrange the stuffed brinjals on top of it. Then cover with the remaining rice. If any shrimps and gravy are left over, put it over the rice. Cover tightly and place on an iron griddle over a medium flame for 15 minutes.

DOSTI PULAO
MACCHLI-CHINGRI-ANDE AUR GUCCHI

• Preparation Time: 35 mins. • Cooking Time: 1 hour • Serves: 8-10

2   gms. saffron
700   gms. basmati rice
3   onions sliced fried
3 ·   bay leaves
4   crushed green cardamoms
2″   stick cinnamon
3   star anise
1   tbsp. ghee
Salt

FOR THE FISH FILLETS

20   small pomfret fillets or any other
       fish
3   sour limes
1   tbsp. black pepper powder
1   tbsp. freshly cut coriander leaves
4-5   eggs
Bread crumbs
Refined oil
Salt

FOR THE PRAWNS

30   fresh medium sized prawn, shelled,
       deveined and washed thrice
8   red chillies   ⎫
½   large pod garlic   ⎪ Grind to a
½″   piece ginger   ⎬ fine paste
1   tsp. cumin seeds   ⎪ with half a
1   tsp. coriander seeds ⎪ cup of
½   tsp. mustard seeds   ⎪ water
18   curry leaves   ⎭
Refined oil
Salt

FOR THE BOILED EGGS

9   eggs boiled each cut into 2
¼   grated fresh coconut   ⎫ Grind in
1   bunch fresh coriander ⎪ ¼ cup of
¼   bunch fresh mint   ⎬ thick
½   tsp. cumin seeds   ⎪ tamarind
1″   fresh ginger   ⎭ water

• Although from the list of things you need for this pulao, the recipe appears daunting — don't worry, it's simple and straight forward. To the inexperienced cook, it will take a little time to get all the items together.

• Cook the rice with saffron, onions, bay leaves, cardamoms, star anise, salt and ghee. When cooked spread on a thali and cool.

• Fry the sliced onions for layering the pulao and keep aside.

• Boil the carrots and potatoes in hot, salted water until tender and drain through a colander and set aside.

• Place the chopped onions in a vessel along with 3 tablespoons of ghee.

• When the cooked onion becomes soft, add the chilli powder, garam masala and the coriander seeds. Lower the flame and add the tomato pulp and bring to a boil. Add the sugar, washed raisins, chopped coriander and the boiled potatoes and carrots. Taste for salt. Allow to simmer for 10 minutes and remove from the fire.

• Wash the fish fillets twice and marinate in salt, lemon juice and black pepper. Sprinkle freshly cut coriander over the fillets so the leaves stick to the fish. Place a karhai half full of refined oil on medium flame. Spread the bread crumbs on a wooden board and coat the fillets on both sides. Whisk the eggs and when the oil heats up, dip each fillet in the eggs and add to the oil. Fry till golden brown and set aside. You will need to fry them in 3 or 4 batches.

Bread crumbs
1 cup gram flour
½ tsp. baking powder
Salt
Oil

FOR THE MUSHROOMS

200 gms. mushrooms soaked in water for ½ hour, sliced and salted
1 tbsp. salted butter

FOR THE LAYERING OF THE PULAO

2 large onions finely chopped
2 large onions sliced
1200 gms. large tomatoes skinned and deseeded
1½ tsps. red reshampatti chilli powder
2 tsps. garam masala
1½ tbsps. sugar
1 tsp. crushed coriander seeds
150 gms. raisins washed
200 gms. carrots cut into small pieces
200 gms. potatoes
½ bunch finely chopped coriander
Salt
Pure ghee

• Wash the prawns thrice. Add salt. Apply the ground masala and keep aside for an hour. Cook the prawns in 2 tablespoons oil and curry leaves and the water with which you wash your grinding stone or mixie. Cook till thick. Taste for salt.

• Cut each of the boiled eggs into two vertical pieces. Coat with the thick chutney paste. Make a batter with 1½ cups of water, salt, baking powder and gram flour, it should not be very thin. Roll each chutney egg piece into the bread crumbs, then dip into the gram flour batter and fry in hot oil. Place the same karhai in which you had fried the fillets. Allow the eggs to become golden red and then remove from the fire and set aside to cool.

• Heat the butter lightly and add the washed, sliced, salted mushrooms. Stir fry for 5 minutes and remove from the fire.

• Take a large biryani vessel. Add some ghee to the bottom of the vessel and spread it over the sides. Divide the rice into four portions. Place one portion at the bottom of the vessel and arrange the fillets on top of the rice.

• Divide the tomato gravy into 3 parts. Sprinkle one portion over the fillets and cover with another layer of rice. Sprinkle all the prawns and the prawn gravy over the rice. Cover with the third layer of rice, and layer the fried eggs over it. Cover with one portion of the tomato gravy. Cover this with the fourth portion of rice and place all the mushrooms over it. Cover the mushrooms with the third portion of the tomato gravy and sprinkle the fried onions. Cover with foil or a tight fitting lid and dough. Place on an iron tava over a medium flame for 30 minutes before serving. This pulao needs no accompaniments except some raw onion kachumber and kulfi with long strands of coloured falooda for dessert.

FRENY'S CHOICE — A PULAO WITH FISH AND PRAWNS

• Preparation Time: 22 mins. • Cooking Time: 1 hour • Serves: 8-10

FOR THE RED RICE

400	gms. rice
3	onions, sliced and deep fried
4	black cardamoms
10	black peppercorns
4	cloves
1"	piece of cinnamon
1	cup tomato ketchup
600	gms. fresh red tomatoes, skinned, deseeded and pulped

Salt
Ghee

FOR THE SAFFRON RICE

100	gms. basmati rice
½	gm. saffron
1	onion sliced and deep fried
2	green cardamoms crushed
½	tsp. carraway seeds
½	tsp. ground coriander seeds

Salt
Ghee

FOR THE FISH

800	gms. pomfret fillets 2" × 2"
16	red kashmiri chillies
1"	fresh ginger chopped
2	large garlic cloves
2	tbsps. broiled cumin seeds
2	tbsps. broiled coriander seeds
1	tsp. black mustard seeds
2"	fresh turmeric if available, if not
1	tsp. turmeric powder
1	tbsp. tamarind cleaned and deseeded
3	onions finely chopped
2	curry sprigs

Grind finely in vinegar

Salt
Ghee

• Add the ketchup to the tomato pulp or juice and measure it. If it comes to less than the quantity for cooking the rice add extra water and make up the deficit. Add to the washed rice in the cooker along with the fried onions, cardamoms, peppercorns, cloves, cinnamon, salt and 1 tablespoon ghee. Cook till tender and empty into a large tray to cool and separate the rice grains.

• Wash the rice cooker, dry it and cook the saffron rice in it. Add saffron heated on an iron griddle and crumbled into half a cup of hot milk, the onion, green cardamoms, coriander seeds, salt and half a tablespoon of ghee. Cook till the rice grains are tender and then spread out in a tray and cool.

• Take the finely chopped onions and place them in a vessel with 2 tablespoons of ghee and cook over a medium flame till soft. Add the curry leaves and cook for 2 more minutes.

• Wash the fillets and salt them. Grind the masala in half a cup of vinegar till soft. Retain the water from washing the grinding stone or mixie.

• Add the masala to the cooked onions and place the vessel on medium heat. Stir for 7 minutes non-stop then add the water you have kept aside and cook till you get thick gravy. Add a little salt. Place the fillets gently in the vessel and shake the vessel from side to side, holding it with 2 kitchen napkins in your hands. Cook till the fillets are done — but are not so soft that they crumble. Remove from the fire. Taste for salt.

• Wash the deveined prawns and salt them. Place the finely chopped spring onions in a vessel with

FOR THE PRAWNS

350	gms. prawns shelled deveined and washed
2	green chillies (not hot type) deseeded
2	tender spring onions
1	cup fresh coriander finely chopped
2	tbsps. mint finely chopped
2	star anise
½	tsp. black pepper powder
1	tsp. mace powder
1	tsp. coarsely ground shahjeera
2	tbsps. sugar

Juice of 2 sour limes
Salt
Ghee

FOR DECORATION

½	cup or more fried ceshewnuts

2 tablespoons of ghee. When soft, add the star anise, pepper powder, mace powder and the shajeera and stir for 2 to 3 minutes. Add deseeded chillies, the salted prawns and stir for 5 minutes. Lower the flame, add 1 cup water and allow to cook till soft. Remove from the fire and stir in the freshly cut coriander, mint, mixed sugar and lemon juice.

- Take a medium sized, tall biryani vessel. Divide the red rice into three parts. Divide the fish fillets and its gravy into 2 portions. Make layers of rice-fish, rice-prawn and then top it all with the saffron rice. Top the saffron rice with fried cashewnuts and seal with a fitting cover and freshly made dough or a tightly fitting foil cover.

- Place the biryani on top of an iron griddle over a medium flame and allow to cook till all the flavours blend, for 20 minutes.

Accompaniments:

Green salad
A baked vegetable dish
Stuffed mango pickle
Dry mince
Bread pudding

HERB, PRAWN AND FISH PULAO

• Preparation Time: 35 mins. • Cooking Time: 55 mins. • Serves: 8-10

FOR THE RICE

500	gms. basmati rice
2	star anise
3	allspice leaves
1	tbsp. butter
Salt	

FOR THE FISH

300	gms. large prawns shelled deveined washed twice
14	small 3" fillets of pomfret, ramas or ghol washed twice
1	kg. tomatoes skinned and pulped
4	spring onions cut julienne
1	pod garlic sliced julienne
1½"	ginger sliced julienne
2	large capsicum sliced julienne
2	tbsps. fresh chopped thyme
2	tbsps. fresh chopped parsley
2	stalks celery cut into 2" pieces
½	cup chopped coriander
Salt	
Butter	

• Cook the rice only with the star anise, all spice leaves, salt and butter in a rice cooker.

• Prawns and the fish fillets should be washed and marinated in salt and set aside.

• Pulp the skinned tomatoes; add the sugar and a pinch of salt.

• Add butter to a wok and place on high heat. Add the spring onions, garlic, ginger, capsicum, thyme, parsley and celery. Make the heat very low. Add the tomato pulp bring to a boil; add the prawns and cook for 15 minutes and then add the fillets and cook for another 12-15 minutes. Taste for salt.

• Place rice in 2 large pyrex dishes then arrange the prawn and fish and the rice in layers. If any fish or prawns are left over, place on top of the rice. Dot with butter and bake for 15 minutes at 350°F.

Accompaniments:

Russian salad

Chilli and tamarind chutney

Fruit salad topped with fresh strawberries and sweet cream

KATY DALAL'S THREE COLOURED VEGETABLE FIESTA

· Preparation Time: 30 mins. · Cooking Time: 1 hour · Serves: 6-8

FOR THE RICE

600 gms. basmati rice
A few drops cochineal colour (pink)
A few drops jalebi colour
A few drops green colour
Salt
Ghee

- Divide the rice into 3 portions of 200 gms. each. Cook each portion separately in a rice cooker with one colour, salt and ghee added.

FOR THE PINK COCHINEAL RICE

For this rice make a mixed vegetable dish and top it with walnuts and sandwich it between two layers of the pink rice.

1	cup grated onions
1	cup skinned chopped tomatoes
1	cup green peas (boiled)
½	cup grated carrots
1	cup finely chopped cauliflower
½	tsp. red chilli powder
½	tsp. turmeric powder
1	tsp. garam masala
1	tsp. sugar

A few broken walnuts
Salt
Ghee

- Place the grated onions in a vessel using 1 tablespoon of ghee on medium heat. Cook till soft and pink and add the chilli, turmeric and garam masala powders. Cook for 2 minutes and add salt and the tomatoes. Lower the flame and add the carrots and the finely chopped cauliflower along with half a cup of water. Cover and allow to cook till soft. Then add the green peas, sugar and mix well and remove from the heat.

FOR THE JALEBI COLOURED RICE

For the filling of this rice, use a mixture of raisins and paneer.

200	gms. paneer
50	gms. raisins
150	gms. skinned chopped tomatoes

A paste of –

4	red chillies deseeded	Grind very fine in 2 tbsps. of water
1	tsp. cumin seeds	
1	tsp. coriander seeds	
10	black peppercorns	
½"	fresh ginger	

A few salted cashewnuts
Salt
Ghee

- Place the chopped tomatoes in a vessel and set aside.

- Chop the paneer into ½" cubes and lightly fry in ghee in a non-stick pan till golden. Drain and set aside. Pour 1 tablespoon of the paneer ghee in the vessel containing the tomatoes. Place over a low flame and allow the tomatoes to cook till soft. Then add the masala paste and cook for 5 minutes. Add half a cup of water and cook for another 5 minutes and when the mixture comes to a boil add the raisins and the salt and the paneer. Mix well and remove from the fire.

FOR THE GREEN RICE

For this rice we have a simple recipe of mushrooms somewhat in Chinese style.

250 gms. sliced mushrooms
8 spring onions from the roots till 6" of greens above them.
4 deseeded green chillies cut fine and diagonally
1" fresh ginger sliced and finely chopped julienne
10 large pods of garlic sliced and cut julienne
½ cup freshly cut thyme
½ cup freshly cut basil
8 dried apricots
A pinch of black pepper powder
Salt
Olive oil or oil or ghee

- Take a wok and pour 1 tablespoon olive oil in it. Heat and add the ginger, garlic and stir. Add the mushrooms and salt and stir. Cook for 5 minutes and then add the spring onions. Lower the heat and cook till the mushrooms are soft. Add the green chillies and the pepper powder, stir for 2 minutes and remove from the heat.

GROUPING THE THREE COLOURED RICE

- Take a salver and place half of all 3 coloured rice in small flat heaps on the base. Cover the pink rice with the vegetable mixture and then the remainder of the pink rice. Top it with broken walnuts.

- Over the jalebi rice place the paneer and raisin mixture and cover it with the remaining jalebi rice. Top with salted whole cashewnuts.

- Over the green rice place the mushroom mixture, cover with the remaining green rice and top with the dried apricots soaked overnight in sugar water.

- Arrange all this whilst the rice and mixture are all hot.

Accompaniments:

Apple and Raisin Raita
Tomato and Cabbage Salan
Cauliflower and Green Peas Salan
Raspberry Jelly with ice-cream

THREE RAW FRUITS PULAO

• Preparation Time: 25 mins. • Cooking Time: 45 mins. • Serves: 10

An extremely unique pulao with unusual taste and an extravagant decoration fit for an important celebration. It consists of raw papaya, semi-ripe mangoes and fresh pineapple cut in decorated rings and then halved. Each of the fruit is cooked separately and placed under a different coloured rice. Hence the pineapple is paired with pink rice, the mangoes with yellow rice and the papaya with white rice mixed with fresh coriander, mint and sautéed cumin.

FOR THE RICE

900 gms. basmati rice
$^1/_2$ cup coriander freshly chopped
2 tbsps. mint freshly chopped
3 tbsps. sugar
Juice of 2 sour limes

PINK RICE

300 gms. basmati rice
5 drops cochineal colour
3 star anise
1 tbsp. ghee
Salt

YELLOW RICE

300 gms. basmati rice
One pinch yellow saffron colour
1 gm. saffron
1 tbsp. ghee
Salt

WHITE RICE

300 gms. basmati rice
1 tbsp. broiled carraway seeds
1 tbsp. ghee
Salt

PINEAPPLE COOKED FOR PINK RICE

450 gms. pineapple grated
200 gms. ambahalad sliced and cut julienne
1 cup fried raisins
2 cups sugar syrup (very light)
4 green chillies cut seedless
$^1/_2$ tbsp. black mustard seeds

• Divide the rice into 3 portions of 300 gms. each. Cook separately in 3 different colours in the rice cooker. Place in a large tray and cool. Mix the sugar with the sour lime juice and sprinkle over the rice. Also sprinkle the chopped coriander and mint.

• Peel the pineapple, grate it and place it in a vessel of water. Drain in a colander.

• Apply a little coarse salt to the pineapple and place it along with the sugar syrup and ambahalad in a vessel and cook over a medium flame till the grated pineapple is ready to eat. Stir well. Add the lime juice.

1   sour lime for juice
1   tbsp. sunflower seed oil
Salt to taste

- Place the oil in a small vessel. Heat it and add the chillies and the mustard seeds to it. Once the seeds pop add the oil to the pineapple and take it off the heat. Allow to cool.

- Mix the raisins into the pink rice.

SEMI-RIPE MANGOES COOKED FOR YELLOW RICE

6   semi-ripe good mangoes, alphonso or pairi
2   onions, finely chopped
1   cup sugar
1   tbsp. red chilli powder
4   green cardamoms roughly crushed in their skins
10   coarsely crushed black peppercorns
½"   cinnamon stick finely crushed
3   cloves finely crushed
1   cup cashewnuts salted broken
A few curry leaves

- Peel and stone the mangoes and cut the flesh into ½" pieces. Place in a vessel of water along with 2 teaspoons of coarse salt.

- Place the oil in a vessel and when hot add the curry leaves and the onions and cook till soft. Drain the mangoes and add them to the onions along with the chilli powder, the cardamoms, cinnamon, cloves and black peppercorns. Stir for 5 minutes and add the sugar and 1 cup of water and bring to the boil. Lower the heat and take the vessel off the fire once the mangoes are soft and the gravy is slightly sticky.

- Mix the fried, salted cashewnuts into the yellow rice.

PAPAYA SLICES COOKED FOR WHITE RICE

1   large semi-ripe papaya peeled and cut into semi-circular slices
2   tbsps. sugar ground
2   large onions finely chopped
1   tbsp. fresh ginger cut julienne
3   curry leaf stems
2   tbsps. garam masala
4   green chillies deseeded and chopped
½   cup fresh coriander chopped
2   tbsps. fresh mint chopped
1   cup pistachios boiled skinned
2   tbsps. sunflower oil
Salt

- Place the papaya slices in 1 cup of water and the ground sugar and cook over a medium fire for 10 minutes.

- Place the ginger and onions along with 1½ tablespoons of sunflower oil in a vessel. Cook over a medium flame till the onions become soft. Add the curry leaves stems, garam masala and chillies and then add the poached papaya slices along with the water till almost all the syrup has dried up. Cook in the onion masala over a low heat till soft. Taste for salt. When papaya slices are soft remove from the fire.

- Mix in the chopped coriander, mint and fried pistaschio slices with the white rice.

TO LAY OUT

- Take a silver salver and place $^2/_3$ of all 3 coloured rice on it. Then place the cooked pineapple on the pink rice and top it with the remaining rice.

- Place the mango mixture over the yellow rice and cover with the remaining rice.

- Place papaya slices over the white rice and cover with the remaining rice.

Accompaniments:

Paneer Curry or Thick Sambhar Dal

Onion and Ginger Chutney

Cabbage Salan

Vanilla Ice-cream with Fresh Figs

RANI KA MAHAL KA BHARELA LAUKI KA PULAO

This year we had a beautiful crop of long, slim, white pumpkins or white gourds. Some of the big ones were 3 kgs. each in weight. For this delicate and delicious recipe take a slim pumpkin, which is very tender, about ten inches long. Cut two inches off the top with the vine attached to it and then carefully remove the thick whitish green skin with a potato peeler. Remove the skin well, grate it and cook it with onions, tomatoes and spices. It comes out very well.

After you have removed the skin cut a hole in the centre of the pumpkin and remove all the pulp that is inside the vegetable. This pulp can be cooked separately as a vegetable along with gram dal. Take a long, thin knife or spoon and hollow out the pumpkin completely. Make the stuffing and fill it to the brim and attach the two inches cut off from the top with its stem and cook it in pure ghee, salt and water.

FOR THE RICE

1	gm. saffron
400	gms. basmati rice
½	tsp. carraway seeds
2	onions sliced and fried
1	tbsp. ghee
Salt	

FOR THE STUFFING

200	gms. onions chopped
200	gms. tomatoes skinned deseeded chopped
200	gms. paneer finely cubed
200	gms. mushrooms finely chopped
100	gms. seedless raisins
100	gms. dried apricots chopped
50	gms. sliced almonds
50	gms. sliced pistachios

• Cook the rice with the saffron, carraway seeds, fried onions, salt and 1 tablespoon of ghee in a rice cooker.

• Cook the stuffing by frying the chopped onions in a large vessel in 1 cup of ghee over a medium flame. Add the finely chopped tomatoes once the onions soften, and then add the finely ground masala. Lower the heat to very low and allow to cook for 5 minutes. Then add the finely chopped paneer and mushroom. Stir and taste for salt. Add the raisins, chopped apricots, almonds and pistachios.

• Place the stuffing in a thali (flat vessel) and mix with bread dipped in water and then squeezed dry or 4 medium mashed potatoes. Taste for salt.

1. Jalebi coloured Rice with Paneer and Raisins
2. Green Rice with Spring Onions and Mushrooms, Chillies and fresh Ginger
3. Pink Cochineal Rice with Cauliflower, Carrots and Green Peas
4. Tamarind and Gaur Chutney
5. Cauliflower and Green Peas Salan

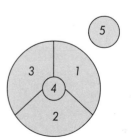

FOR THE GROUND MASALA

3   green chillies deseeded
3   red dry chillies deseeded
6   black peppercorns   Grind
½"   cinnamon   fine
1   tsp. coriander seeds   in a
½   tsp. cumin seeds   little
½   cup coriander freshly   water
       chopped
1   tbsp. mint freshly chopped
6   slices of stale bread or 4 mashed
       potatoes

Salt
Ghee

FOR THE DECORATION

4   sheets of silver-vark

- Stuff the above mixture tightly into the hollowed out pumpkin and take the 2" of the top which was cut off with the stem and replace it on the vegetable with the help of toothpicks.

- Take a large vessel and place 1 cup ghee and 4 cups water in it. Add sufficient salt for the pumpkin to cook well. When the water boils place the pumpkin in it. Cover tightly and cook over a medium flame. Turn it over several times, and when necessary, keep adding cups of hot water till the vegetable becomes soft and tender. This will take well over an hour.

- Remove the hot rice onto a flat dish and place the vegetable and its gravy over the rice. Slice the pumpkin along with portions of rice. Cover with the sliver-vark.

Accompaniments:

Thick dal

Potato raita

Hot mango pickle

Rabri with rasmalai

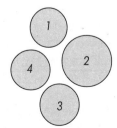

1. *Pink rice with pineapple*
2. *Semi-ripe mangoes with yellow rice*
3. *Semi-ripe Papaya with white rice*
4. *Vegetable Pakoras*

STUFFED SNAKE GOURD VEGETABLE PULAO

• Preparation Time: 30 mins. • Cooking Time: 1 hour • Serves: 6-10

FOR THE RICE

900 gms. basmati rice
2 crisply fried onions
One pinch yellow pulao colour
Salt

FOR THE SNAKE GOURD

2-3 very tender snake gourds well prepared by cleaning the surface of its white thin flaky skin. Cut into 3" pieces from the thick portions only. Discard the rest or use the pieces for making a vegetable dish.
400 gms. mashed potatoes
300 gms. finely chopped onions
100 gms. grated carrots
100 gms. freshly grated coconut
100 gms. coarsely chopped cashewnuts
2 sour limes for juice
1 tsp. amchur powder
1 cup chopped fresh coriander
3 sprigs curry leaves
1½ tsp. mustard seeds
Coconut or any other refined oil

FOR THE GROUND MASALA

10	cashewnuts	
6	green chillies deseeded	To be
1	tbsp. broiled cumin	ground
1	tbsp. broiled coriander seeds	with a little
1	large pod garlic	water
¼	coconut grated	

EXTRAS

4-6 bread slices
Gram flour
Breadcrumbs

• Cook the rice along with the fried onions, salt and 1 to 2 tablespoons ghee in a rice cooker. Do not add the colour.

• Clean and cut the snake gourd and remove the soft spongy insides. Wash and place in aluminium, stainless steel or copper sieve, sprinkle with salt and steam the pieces. Cover with a cloth or lid till tender but firm.

• Take a large vessel and place the finely chopped onions in it along with the mustard seeds, a cup of oil, curry leaves and cook till soft. Then add the grated carrots and coconut and lower the flame and cook for 5 minutes stirring all the time. Add the masala and stir for another 7 minutes. Add the masala water from the grinding stone or the mixie, as well as the cashew nuts, lime juice, amchur powder, and the chopped, fresh coriander leaves and mix well.

• Finally add the mashed potatoes to the mixture and stir up and down. Taste for salt. After 5 minutes remove the potato mixture from the fire.

• Stuff the snake gourds with the mixture. Make a thin solution of gram flour, salt and water. Dip little pieces of bread from the centre of the slices into the solution and use them to plug both the cut sides of the snake gourd pieces.

• Take a large vessel and fill it halfway with oil. Heat on a high flame and when the oil is hot, lower the flame a little and dip each piece in the batter and fry the gourd in small batches. Fry till golden in colour and set out in a thali.

• If any potato mixture is left over make tiny balls of it and dip in the batter and deep fry.

- Place the hot rice on a flat dish and stud it with the pieces of fried gourd and decorate with the small balls, if any are there.

Accompaniments:

Dal or Tomato Gravy with Vegetables in a Hot Sour Sauce

Sweet Banana Raita

Beetroot and Carrot Salad

Water Melon Ice-cream

BENGALI BAHU KHUDA PULAO
(The Hungry Bride's Pulao)

- Preparation Time: 10 mins. • Cooking Time: 50 mins. • Serves: 8

This is an interesting name for a rice dish. Since the wives had to eat last or not at all if all the food was over, this dish was invented for self-gratification. It was very simple and could be cooked fast if it got over and so the new bride or wife was not deprived of her share of the meal. I don't know how many Indians would take to pulao rice being cooked in mustard oil. I would suggest pure ghee if you have any hesitation in using mustard oil.

700	gms. jeera sal rice
6	large onions sliced
6	green long chillies slit and deseeded
1	cup fresh coriander chopped
½	cup fresh mint chopped
1	tbsp. coriander seeds broiled, coarsely ground
10	peppercorns coarsely ground

A pinch of turmeric

Mustard oil or pure ghee

- Deep fry the onions in ghee or mustard oil till golden brown and crisp. Set aside.

- Cook your rice in the rice cooker. Add a little, about one-fourth of the fried onions, the slit green chillies, coarsely ground coriander, black peppercorns, turmeric, salt and 2 tablespoons of pure ghee. Cook till the rice is tender and fluffy.

- Remove the rice into a salver and sprinkle the top completely with the crisp fried onions and the freshly chopped coriander and mint.

Accompaniments:

Mutton Gravy Dish, Fried Prawns

Red and white Radish in lime juice, salt and green chillies

Rasagoollas

AFGHANI ALOO KA PULAO

- Preparation Time: 20 mins. • Cooking Time: 1 hour • Serves: 8-10

FOR THE RICE

2	gms. saffron
800	gms. basmati rice
2	onions sliced and fried crisp
2	(1") pieces cinnamon
3	star anise
3	large brown cardamom
4	bay leaves

Salt
Pure ghee

FOR THE POTATOES

1¼ kg. large elongated potatoes
You should have atleast 6-8 potatoes
Salt
Ghee

FOR THE MARINATION

200	gms. thick curd
8	kashmiri dried chillies — paste
1	tbsp. ginger-garlic paste
1	tbsp. broiled cumin seeds powder
1½	tsps. garam masala
1	tsp. dried kasoori methi

Salt

FOR THE STUFFING

300	gms. paneer cubed
100	gms. potatoes boiled cubed
50	gms. almonds boiled skinned crushed
50	gms. pistachios boiled skinned crushed
100	gms. raisins
1	tbsp. minced fresh ginger
1	cup finely chopped coriander and mint
4	cardamoms deseeded finely powdered
1	tsp. pomegranate seeds
1	tsp. garam masala

- Take large elongated potatoes. Wash well. Cut into 2 pieces and scoop out the insides. Soak in salted water. Boil the scooped potatoes to use for the filling.

- Dry the cut, scooped potatoes. Heat a karahi half filled with oil and place on medium heat. Deep fry the potatoes, a few at a time till golden brown. Set aside.

- Meanwhile fry the onions crisp, the cinnamon, star anise, cardamoms, bay leaves and the rice in 2 tablespoons of pure ghee. Stir over medium heat for 5 minutes, add salt and place in the rice cooker till tender and fluffy.

- Place all the stuffing materials in a thali and mix gently. Heat a frying pan with 2 tablespoons of ghee and place over medium to low flame and stir carefully for 5 minutes. Cool and stuff the potatoes with this mixture.

- Prepare the marinade by mixing all the ingredients in a flat bottomed, wide mouthed vessel. Add salt and mix well and smear the potatoes with the mixture. Rest the potatoes in the vessel itself for an hour to absorb the marinate.

- Next take the vessel and place on a low flame and allow the vessel to get hot for a minute or two. Then mix all the gravy items well and add to the vessel a little at a time. Do not totally submerge the potatoes in the gravy. Cover and cook on the lowest flame possible taking care to see that the vessel does not burn at the centre. When all the thick gravy has been used up, cover the pan and remove from the fire. This process will take 30-40 minutes.

2 tbsps. chaat masala
2 tbsps. pure ghee

FOR THE GRAVY

700 gms. tomatoes skinned pulped
100 gms. apples skinned cored pulped
1 tsp. shahjeera seeds
½ cup tomato sauce for colour
½ tsp. cardamom powder
½ tsp. cinnamon powder
1 tbsp. sugar
Salt

• Grease a large biryani vessel at the bottom and sides and make 3 layers of the rice and potatoes. Use up all the gravy. Cover with a tight lid and dough. Place on an iron tava over a medium flame for 30 minutes for all the lovely aromas of the cardamoms, shahjeera and apples to blend together.

Accompaniments:

Salad of Fresh Fruits and Vegetables

Sweet Curd or Yogurt

Ladyfinger Vegetable

Almond Halwa

SHALIMAR KE MAKHANE PULAO

• Preparation Time: NIL • Cooking Time: 35 mins. • Serves: 4-6

300 gms. basmati rice
250 gms. lotus seeds
3 large onions chopped
2 large tomatoes chopped
3 green chillies deseeded and chopped
10 garlic cloves chopped
1 tbsp. chopped ginger
1 tbsp. crushed cumin
1 tbsp. dried ginger powder
4 cloves
1 pinch asafoetida
Salt
Ghee

• Boil the lotus seeds for 20 minutes, cool and skin them. Set them aside.

• Cook the chopped onions in 2 tablespoons of ghee. When soft and pink, add the green chillies, garlic, chopped ginger, crushed cumin, ginger powder, cloves and asafoetida and stir gently over a medium heat till all the spices have been well cooked in the ghee. This should take 5 minutes. Add the skinned lotus seeds and lower the flame and cook for 5 minutes more. Add the salt, washed rice and water and tip the whole mixture into the rice cooker till rice is tender and soft.

• Serve with a hot chicken curry.

VEGETABLE KHEEMA MUTTER PULAO

• Preparation Time: 25 mins. • Cooking Time: 55 mins. • Serves: 6-8

FOR THE RICE

400	gms. rice long grained
2	sliced onions fried crisp
1"	cinnamon
4	green cardamoms crushed
3	bay leaves
1	tbsp. ghee

Pinch of saffron colour
Salt

FOR THE MINCED VEGETABLES

200	gms. green peas boiled in salt and Soda bicarb water
150	gms. paneer crushed lightly
100	gms. mushrooms minced
100	gms. carrots minced
100	gms. cabbage minced
400	gms. tomatoes skinned and chopped
250	gms. onions finely chopped
1/2	cup coriander chopped
2	tbsps. mint chopped
2"	fresh ginger grated
3	sprigs curry leaves
1 1/2	tsps. turmeric powder
1 1/2	tsps. chilli powder
2	tsps. dry pomegranate seeds
1	tsp. dried ginger powder
2	tsps. garam masala
2	tsps. ground fennel seeds
2	tsps. coriander seeds
2	tsps. cumin seeds

Salt
Ghee

• Cook the rice along with the sliced, fried onions, cinnamon, cardamoms, bay leaves, salt and ghee in a rice cooker. When the rice is ready, melt the colour in half a cup of water and sprinkle it over half the rice so it turns saffron. Set aside.

• Place the chopped onions in a large vessel with 1/2 cup ghee over medium heat. Cook till soft and pink. Add grated ginger and curry sprigs. Cook for 2 more minutes and add the minced carrots and cabbage. When cooked add the mushrooms, tomatoes and sprinkle turmeric and chilli powder, dried ginger powder, garam masala, and the pomegranate seeds. Stir well for 2 minutes. Add the ground fennel seeds, coriander seeds and cumin seeds. Add 1/2 cup of water and cover with a lid. Add water to the lid and cook over very low heat till the vegetable is cooked. Add salt. Stir and taste.

• Add the green peas and crushed paneer as well as coriander and mint to the vegetables, stirring gently.

• Take a large vessel. Grease its sides and bottom well. Place the white rice at the bottom. On top of it place the minced vegetables and then the saffron rice. Cover with a tight lid and place on a low fire for 15 minutes. Serve with lime pickle and sweet yogurt.

Accompaniments:

Fenugreek Bhaji
Sweet Stuffed Tomatoes
Cucumber Salad
Fresh Figs with Ice-cream

COCONUT AND VEGETABLE PULAO

• Preparation Time: 25 mins. • Cooking Time: 55 mins. • Serves: 10

700	gms. basmati rice	
100	gms. small carrots sliced	
100	gms. small potatoes sliced	
150	gms. green peas	
1	capsicum cut julienne	
3	bay leaves	
Milk of 2 coconuts		
Juice of 2 sour limes		Mix
2	tsps. sugar	together
2	large onions chopped	
3	bay leaves	
5	boiled eggs	
3	dried red chillies deseeded	
1"	piece ginger	Grind
1	tbsp. broiled coriander seeds	to a paste
½	cup chopped coriander leaves	in a little water
½	tsp. cumin	
1	tsp. turmeric	
1	cup broken or whole cashewnuts salted and fried	
Salt		
Ghee		

• Parboil the sliced carrots and potatoes and set aside. Half cook the green peas in salted water. Add a pinch of soda bicarb to it and drain in a colander. Set aside.

• Take the chopped onions and place them in a large vessel. Add 3 tablespoons of ghee and cook the onions till soft and pink. Add the bay leaves. Remove the vessel from the fire.

• Grind the masala very fine and mix it with the amount of coconut milk you will need to cook the rice with.

• Replace the vessel with the cooked onions on the fire and when they get hot gently add the sliced carrots, potatoes and peas and shake the vessel from side to side. If desired, add 1 more tablespoon of ghee to it. Then after 5 minutes gently add the washed rice to the vegetables as well as salt and cook the rice for 5 minutes more. Transfer the rice to the rice cooker and then add the coconut milk with the masala mixed into it. Taste for salt and switch on the cooker till the rice is tender. Open the cooker lid, pour in the sour lime and sugar and close the lid at once.

• Remove to a flat dish whilst still hot and decorate the sides with the boiled eggs. Sprinkle the top with the cashewnuts.

Accompaniments:

Potato and Nut Vegetable

Salad of Spring Onions and Capsicums

Mango Pickle and Fried/Roasted Papads

Green and Red Almond Halwas

CHEESE VEGETABLES AND RED RICE PULAO

• Preparation Time: 12 mins. • Cooking Time: 40 mins. • Serves: 6-8

FOR THE RICE

400	gms. basmati rice
2	onions chopped and fried in ghee
3	bay leaves
3	cardamoms crushed
2	(1") pieces cinnamon
1	tsp. carraway seeds
1½	cups tomato sauce
1	tbsp. ghee
Salt	

FOR THE VEGETABLES

100	gms. tiny potatoes cubed boiled
100	gms. tiny carrots cubed boiled
100	gms. french beans cubed boiled
100	gms. green peas boiled
100	gms. cauliflower broken into small florets boiled
3	medium sized onions
4	large tomatoes chopped fine
½	bunch parsley, finely chopped
8	green chillies deseeded
1	tsp. garam masala
1	tsp. mace
1	tbsp. chopped garlic
1	tbsp. minced ginger
3	tbsps. ghee
Salt	

FOR THE TOPPING

200	gms. grated cheese

• Place the washed rice, chopped fried onions, bay leaves, cardamoms, cinnamon and carraway seeds in the rice cooker. Add the tomato sauce and sufficient water to cook the rice. Add salt and the ghee and cook rice till tender. Place in a thali to cool and separate the grains.

• Boil each of the vegetables separately till crisp. They should not be very soft. Chop the onions finely and place them in a vessel along with the ghee. Cook over a medium flame till golden brown and add the green chillies, mace, garam masala, ginger and garlic. Mix for 3 to 5 minutes and then add the tomatoes and cook till soft. Add half the finely chopped parsley, and the boiled vegetables. Stir for 5 minutes. The vegetables will release water. Cook over a slow fire and taste for salt. When the water dries up remove the vessel from the fire. Mix well.

• Divide the rice into 2 portions. Place one at the base of a large vessel and make a second layer with the vegetables. Cover with the remaining rice and top with the remaining parsley and all the cheese. Bake at 350°F for 20 minutes and serve hot.

TANSEN MIA KA MEWA AUR TARKARI PULAO

• Preparation Time: 20 mins. • Cooking Time: 55 mins. • Serves: 10

FOR THE RICE

2	gms. saffron
700	gms. basmati rice
3	onions sliced, fried
100	gms. pink masoor dal washed
4	bay leaves
2"	piece of cinnamon
3	bruised green cardamoms
3	mace flowers
2	star anise

Salt
Pure ghee

FOR THE VEGETABLES

300	gms. small carrots cleaned cubed boiled
300	gms. small frenchbeans cleaned cubed boiled
300	gms. small sweet potatoes cleaned cubed boiled
300	gms. small ladyfingers cleaned cubed fried
300	gms. small red pumpkin cleaned cubed fried
500	gms. tomatoes skinned pulped
500	gms. onions finely chopped
1	bunch fresh coriander finely cut
½	cup mint finely chopped
½	bunch dill washed and finely cut
2	tbsps. broiled ground coriander seeds
2	tbsps. garam masala
1½	tbsps. red chilli powder
1½	tsps. turmeric
1	tsp. mace ground
1	tsp. nutmeg ground
1	tsp. green cardamom seeds ground
1	tsp. fennel ground
1	tsp. powdered dry ginger

Salt
Pure ghee

• Make the rice in the rice cooker along with the saffron, fried onions, masoor dal, bay leaves, cinnamon, cardamoms, mace, star anise, salt and ghee. When cooked spread out in a thali to cool.

• Take a large vessel and cook the finely chopped onions in 3 tablespoons of ghee. When cooked to a light golden colour, add the pulped tomatoes, ground coriander, garam masala, chilli powder, turmeric, mace, nutmeg, cardamom, fennel and powdered dry ginger. Stir and add the boiled carrots, frenchbeans and sweet potatoes as well as the fried ladyfingers and pumpkin. Mix gently and add the fresh mint and fresh coriander and allow to simmer, covered over a low heat for 5 to 7 minutes. Taste for salt.

• Take a large non-stick frying pan. Add 1 tablespoon pure ghee or more as required and add all the nuts to it. Stir rapidly till a light golden brown. Add all the fruits and lower the heat and stir gently until the nuts and fruits have mixed well.

• Mix the rice with the rose petals. Take a large vessel, preferably a biryani top. Grease the bottom and sides generously with pure ghee. Put a little vegetable mixture to line the bottom of the dish. Spread a layer of rice. Keep some nuts and fruits aside. Cover the rice with a vegetable layer. Then add a layer of nuts. Spread the rice again

FOR THE MEWA

NUTS

1	cup salted roasted cashewnuts
1	cup salted roasted almonds
1	cup salted roasted pistachios
½	cup salted roasted peanuts
¼	cup water melon seeds
¼	cup cucumber seeds

Salt
Ghee

FRUITS

½	cup golden raisins washed
½	cup black raisins washed
½	cup dried figs soaked overnight in sugar water
½	cup dried apricots soaked overnight in sugar water

Salt
Pure ghee

FOR THE DECORATION

4	sheets silver vark
2	red apples — cut into 4 and cored
½	cup pink rose petals

and top with the vegetables and then a layer of nuts and fruits. Top with the rice and the remainder of the nuts and fruits. Cover with silver foil and place a lid on the vessel. Seal the lid with fresh dough. Place on an iron tava over a medium flame for 20 minutes to allow all the aromas to assimilate.

- Decorate with the apple pieces and serve with a hot dal, fresh spring onions, sliced cucumbers, radish, capsicum and lettuce.

Accompaniments:

Cooked brinjal
Tendli bhaji
Chilli pickle

SWEET CORN PULAO

• Preparation Time: 15 mins. • Cooking Time: 40 mins. • Serves: 8

FOR THE RICE

400	gms basmati rice
4	crushed green cardamom
1	tsp. carraway seeds
3	bay leaves
10	black pepper corns
3	onions sliced, deep fried

FOR THE GREEN LAYER

2	bunches spring onions
8	green chillies deseeded and cut fine
1	bunch spinach leaves
1	tbsp. chopped garlic
1	tbsp. chopped fresh ginger
1	tbsp. cumin ground
3	tbsps. sugar

Juice of 3 sour limes

FOR THE SWEET CORN LAYER

2	corns of green giant corn niblets
3	cups milk
2	tbsps. maida
1	tbsp. sugar

Salted butter
Pinches of cinnamon and pepper powders
Salt
Oil
Pure ghee

• Cook the rice with the ingredients.

• Wash and finely chop the spinach leaves and the spring onions. Do not use coarse onion leaves and spinach stems.

• Heat 2 tablespoons pure ghee and when hot, add the ground cumin, green chillies, garlic and ginger. Stir for 2 minutes and add the finely chopped spinach and spring onions. Cook over a very low flame, and avoid getting a dark colour for the leaves. Stir for 5 minutes and add sugar and lemon juice. Mix for 3 more minutes and remove from the fire.

• Place 100 gms. butter in a saucepan. Add maida and stir over a very low flame. Add the milk and make a thin white sauce. Drain the corn in a colander and add to the white sauce along with the sugar. Taste for salt. Sprinkle the cinnamon and pepper powder and mix well.

• Divide the rice into 2 and place 1 portion on the bottom of a large pyrex dish or vessel. Cover it with all the spinach and green spring onion layer. Smoothen it and spread the buttered corn in white sauce and cover with the remaining rice. Cover with foil. If using a pyrex dish bake in an oven at 325°F for 20 minutes. If using a vessel place on an iron tava for 15 minutes over a medium flame.

Accompaniments:

Hot tomato gravy
Stuffed brinjals
Parathas
Caramel custard

STUFFED LADYFINGER PULAO

· Preparation Time: 20 mins. · Cooking Time: 45 mins. · Serves: 8

FOR THE RICE

2	gms. saffron
400	gms. basmati rice
4	bay leaves
2	onions sliced fried
1	tsp. shahjeera broiled
1	tsp. nigelle seeds broiled
3	cloves
3	green cardamoms

FOR THE LADYFINGERS

25	tender ladyfingers washed with their heads cut off
1	cup gram flour
1	onion minced
½	bunch large fenugreek leaves
½	bunch fresh coriander leaves
1	tsp. fresh mint leaves chopped
2	green chillies deseeded and finely chopped
1	tsp. cumin powder
1	tsp. dried ginger powder
½	tsp. mustard seeds powder
½	tsp. red chillies powder
2	tbsps. sugar
	Juice of 2 sour limes

} Mix together

Salt
Oil
Pure ghee

· Cook the rice along with the saffron, bay leaves, shahjeera seeds, nigelle seeds, cloves, cardamoms, fried onions, 1 tablespoon pure ghee and salt.

· Slit each ladyfinger from top to bottom, half way only. Not through and through.

· Place the gram flour into a bowl. Wash the coriander and fenugreek leaves and then dry them with a kitchen napkin. Cut or crush them finely and add to the gram flour. Add the minced onion, chillies, mint and salt. Mix the flour with a spoon. Add the spice powders, cumin, ginger, mustard seeds and red chilli powder. Add salt to taste. Mix in the sour lime juice and sugar and stir the mixture, pouring in a slow stream of water till the flour is stiff and sticky and will not run off the ladyfinger.

· Take one ladyfinger at a time and stuff each with the wet flour mixture with your index finger. Fill well.

· Half fill a karhai with refined oil and deep fry the stuffed ladyfingers. Remove onto a colander.

· Place the hot rice in a serving dish and arrange the hot ladyfingers onto the rice. Lightly mix the major portion into the rice and serve hot with lime pickle in oil.

MUTTER PULAO

- Preparation Time: 7 mins. • Cooking Time: 45 mins. • Serves: 8

FOR THE RICE

300	gms. long grained rice
2	large onions sliced and deep fried
1	tsp. carraway seeds
3	large black cardamoms
3	star anise
Salt	
Ghee	

FOR THE VEGETABLES

200	gms. green peas
200	gms. onions finely chopped
200	gms. tomatoes skinned, finely chopped
1½	cups fresh coriander finely chopped
2	tbsps. fresh mint finely chopped
1	large carrot scraped and finely chopped
1½"	ginger piece freshly crushed
6	large cloves garlic freshly crushed
1	tsp. garam masala
150	gms. mawa or khoya
Salt	
Ghee	

FOR THE DECORATION

15-20 whole fried cashewnuts

- Prepare the rice with salt, sliced fried onion, carraway seeds, black cardamoms and star anise in a rice cooker. Also add the finely cut carrot and 1 tablespoon ghee.

- If using frozen peas immerse in water and bring them to room temperature. Drain in a colander.

- Place the chopped onion and 2 tablespoons ghee in a vessel. Allow the onions to cook till soft and pink, add the green peas, ginger and garlic and 2 cups of hot water. Add more water if the green peas do not become tender by the time the water evaporates.

- When the green peas are soft add the mawa after crushing it and cook over a very, very slow fire till it mingles and melts into the peas. Add the tomatoes, coriander and mint and cover and cook till the tomato is pulped. Taste for salt. Sprinkle the garam masala, mix well and remove from the fire.

- Once the rice is cooked mix it lightly so the grains separate. Place the rice and green peas in layers in a vessel. Start with rice and end with rice. Cover tightly with foil and place on an iron tava over a medium flame for 15 minutes.

- Decorate with the cashewnuts.

Accompaniments:

Hot coconut curry
Raw green salad of cabbage and beetroots
Sweet mango chutney.

NAVRATNA VEGETABLE PULAO

● Preparation Time: 25 mins. ● Cooking Time: 55 mins. ● Serves: 6-8

FOR THE RICE

2	gms. saffron
600	gms. basmati rice.
2	onions sliced fried crisp
3	large brown cardamoms
3	star anise
1	cup milk
1	tbsp. ghee
Salt	

FOR THE VEGETABLES

150	gms. fresh green peas boiled with salt and a pinch of soda bicarb
150	gms. onions finely chopped
100	gms. carrots cut into ½" cubes
100	gms. capsicums cut into ½" cubes
100	gms. potatoes cut into ½" cubes
50	gms. frenchbeans cut into ½" pieces
50	gms. cauliflower cut into ½" florets

FOR THE GROUND MASALA

3	green chillies deseeded
3	red chillies deseeded
2	tbsps. dried coriander seeds
2	tbsps. fennel seeds
4	green cardamoms seeds only
4	mace flowers
1	tbsp. shahjeera
1"	cinnamon
6	cloves
10	peppercorns

Grind in a little water

FOR THE DECORATION

100	gms. whole small cashewnuts
100	gms. large dried raisins
300	gms. skinned tomatoes
100	gms. apples peeled, cubed
200	gms. canned or fresh pineapple cubes

● Cook the rice with the fried onions, large cardamoms, star anise, salt and pure ghee. Meanwhile roast the saffron lightly on an iron tawa and steep in half a cup of hot water. When the rice is ready separate it into two portions. Pinch the saffron in the water and then pour it over one half of the rice and mix well.

● Place the finely chopped onions in a large vessel with 1 cup of ghee. Allow the onion to turn pink and soft and add the ground masala and stir non-stop for 5 minutes. Add salt and the tomatoes and lower the heat and cook for 5 minutes. Then add the chopped washed carrots, potatoes, frenchbeans and cauliflower. Cover the vessel with a well fitting lid, pour water on the lid and cook over a low fire. Keep checking the vessel to see it does not burn, keep adding hot water from the lid replacing the water on the lid. When almost done, add the boiled green peas, the canned or fresh pineapple, the capsicum and the cut apples and mix gently. Remove from the fire after 5 minutes. Mix in the freshly chopped coriander and the whipped curd when the vegetables cool. Also mix in the paneer. Do not fry it.

● Take a small saucepan and heat one cup of milk. Add a pinch of salt and the mawa finely crumbled and stir vigorously till there are no crumbs. Remove from the fire and set aside.

● Grease a large vessel all over with pure ghee. Place one portion of the rice which is plain and cover it with a thick layer of the vegetables. Cover with the saffron rice. Pour the heated mawa over the rice. Cover the vessel with a tight fitting lid and dough. Place an iron tava over a

100 gms. mawa
200 gms. thick curd
200 gms. best full cream paneer cubed
1 cup fresh coriander chopped

medium flame for 25 minutes. Allow to rest for 7 minutes.

- Fry the large raisins in ghee till they become fluffy. Remove from the ghee and in the same pan fry the cashewnuts till golden in colour.

- Remove the pulao on a large dish and decorate with the fried raisins and the cashewnuts.

KHUMBI KA MALAI-KESAR PULAO

Preparation Time: 10 mins. • Cooking Time: 35 mins. • Serves: 6-8

FOR THE RICE

500 gms. basmati rice
800 gms. washed sliced mushrooms
200 gms. cream
3 onions sliced and deep fried
1 tsp. carraway seeds coarsely ground
1 tsp. coriander seeds coarsely ground
1 tsp. black pepper corns coarsely ground
3 tbsps. fresh coriander finely chopped
2 tbsps. fresh mint finely chopped
4 green chillies deseeded and finely chopped
4 tsps. salted butter
Salt

- Wash the rice and set aside.

- Place the butter in a vessel and sauté the mushrooms till they are half cooked. Add the carraway seeds, coriander seeds, peppercorns and salt and cook for 5 minutes. Add the fried onions, rice and water and place it all in a rice cooker.

- Once the rice is cooked place it in a serving dish, pour over lightly beaten cream and sprinkle over the coriander, mint and green chillies.

Accompaniment:

Raita with Onion and Fresh Grapes
Fried Potatoes-Ladyfingers
Hot Lime Pickle
Ripe figs in syrup and cream

RAW BABY MANGOES, BABY ONIONS AND BABY POTATO PULAO

Preparation Time: 12-15 mins. • Cooking Time: 30 mins. • Serves: 6

FOR THE VEGETABLES

300	gms. baby potatoes
300	gms. baby onions
200	gms. baby raw mangoes
300	gms. finely chopped onions
20	gms. finely chopped garlic
20	gms. finely chopped ginger
8	deseeded and finely chopped chillies
½	cup coriander freshly cut
3	sprigs curry leaves
4	sprigs mint leaves and stalks finely chopped
Salt	
Oil	

FOR THE MASALA

200	gms. grated coconut	
100	gms. roasted peanuts	Grind fine in ½ cup water
10	black peppercorns	
10	allspice corns (kababchini)	
12	kashmiri chillies	

FOR THE RICE

300	gms. basmati rice
3	bay leaves
¼	tsp. nutmeg powder
1	tsp. nigelle seeds
1	tsp. cumin seeds
½	tsp. mustard seeds
6	crushed green cardamoms
Salt	
Ghee	

• Peel the onions, potatoes and mangoes and place into salted water.

• Place 70 grams ghee in a vessel and when hot add the bay leaves, nigelle, cumin and mustard seeds and the cardamoms. Fry for 5 minutes. Add the washed rice and salt and cook in a rice cooker till tender.

• Place the chopped onions and 3 tablespoons oil in a large vessel. Stir the onions and allow to cook till soft. Lower the flame and add the salt, chopped garlic, ginger, green chillies, coriander and curry sprigs. Cook for 5 minutes and add the potatoes and onions and 2 cups water and half cook them. Then add the mangoes. When the vegetables are soft add the ground masala and cook for 12-15 minutes. Taste for salt. Sprinkle the mint on top of the gravy.

• Take a large flat bottomed vessel and sandwich the potato, onion and mango gravy between two layers of rice. Cover tightly and place on dum for 10 minutes.

• Serve with fried fresh or dried fish or with papads and chutney.

1. *Mutter Pulao*
2. *Raita with Onions and Coriander*
3. *Mushroom Pulao*
4. *Hot Carrot and Fruit Pickle*

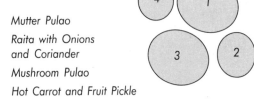

IYENGAR VEN PONGAL PULAO WITH TAMARIND GOJJU (SAUCE)

• Preparation Time: 5 mins. • Cooking Time: 45-55 mins. • Serves: 6-8

FOR THE RICE

600 gms. rice
375 gms. mung dal
3 bay leaves
Salt

FOR TASTE

10 black peppercorns coarsely crushed
2½ tsps. broiled cumin coarsely crushed
3" piece dried kopra grated
1 cup broken cashewnuts fried
2 sprig curry leaves
Pure ghee

TAMARIND GOJJU

2 cups tamarind water
1 cup grated jaggery
4 red chillies dried deseeded
1 tsp. mustard seeds
½ tsp. fenugreek seeds
1½ tbsps. coconut oil
1 sprig curry leaves

• Wash the rice and dal well and cook along with the bay leaves and salt in the rice cooker.

• Once the rice-dal mixture is cooked till soft, gently mix in the black peppercorns, cumin and the fried cashewnuts. Heat the grated kopra gently on an iron tava and add it to the rice.

• Heat half a cup or more of pure ghee. Pour it over the rice and mix it in gently.

• Serve hot with tamarind gojju.

• Boil the jaggery and tamarind water till it thickens. Strain and pour into a clean bowl.

• Heat the oil in a karhai and when hot, drop in the curry sprigs, mustard and fenugreek seeds and the red dried chillies.

• Pour the hot oil with spices into the tamarind jaggery mixture and serve with the rice and dal.

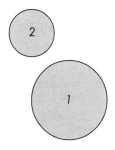

1. *Stuffed Chilli Pulao*
2. *Orange Rind Raita*

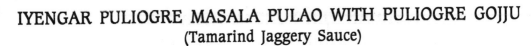

IYENGAR PULIOGRE MASALA PULAO WITH PULIOGRE GOJJU
(Tamarind Jaggery Sauce)

• Preparation Time: 5 mins. • Cooking Time: 45 mins. • Serves: 6-8

FOR THE RICE

600	gms. rice
2	star anise
4	bay leaves
Salt	
Pure ghee	

FOR TASTE AND MASALA

1	cup dried peanuts
2	cups puliogre gojju liquid
1½	tsps. mustard seeds
2	sprigs curry leaves
2	tbsps. grated dried kopra
1	tbsp. black sesame seeds broiled and powdered
2	tbsps. sugar
Salt	
Ghee	

PULIOGRE GOJJU

1	cup tamarind
3	cups grated best quality jaggery
10	curry leaves
2	tbsps. rasam powder
2	tbsps. sesame seeds broiled and powdered
Salt	

• Cook the rice along with the star anise, bay leaves, salt and 1 tablespoon pure ghee in a rice cooker.

• Heat 1 tablespoon ghee in a frying pan, place on medium heat and drop in the mustard seeds, peanuts, curry leaves and mix into the rice.

• Lightly roast the grated kopra and add it to the rice along with the sesame powder and sugar. Taste for salt. Heat 1 more tablespoon ghee and pour onto the rice along with puliogre gojju liquid. Mix and serve hot.

• Boil the tamarind in two cups of water till it has become very soft. Squeeze it through a fine strainer and pour it into a sauce pan. Add the crushed jaggery and boil to a thick sauce.

• Take 1 tablespoon peanut oil and heat it in a frying pan. Add the curry leaves, rasam powder, and sesame powder along with salt, and stir this mixture into the jaggery-tamarind mixture.

RAJASTHANI GATTA PULAO

- Preparation Time: 20 mins. • Cooking Time: 1 hour • Serves: 10

Since the last fifty years, because of the various canal projects, the sands of the deserts of Rajasthan have turned into a paradise. There are miles of mustard fields to be seen and fruit orchards which yield huge quantities of oranges and pomegranates. In the cold weather, the farms on either side of the canal yield huge white cauliflowers, the tenderest of green cabbages, huge red, sugary carrots and the largest green peas pods I have ever seen. But in other parts where irrigation canals do not exist, conditions are very bad and the village people live on cereals, dals and dehydrated vegetables. They depend on milk products from their cattle to a large extent. The snack items are mainly made out of grains and dals. Papads play a very important role in Rajasthani cuisine. You have masala papads, roast papads, stuffed papads, rice mangodis, rice bhajias, fried kachori and dried guvarphalli. There is heavy dependence on ker, sangri and kumat. As far as vegetables go, one favourite item is dried sangar which is soaked, boiled and cooked. They go in for a lot of pickles which can be eaten with rice and rotlas as well as chutneys.

One very famous Rajasthani dish is dal batti. There is a legion of parathas, rotlas, puris, and dal preparations. Every meal consists of a dal dish cooked as a gravy dish or soaked or ground and made into a sweet, a bhajia or a side dish.

A batti is a dumpling made out of wheat flour or gram flour, mixed with a little rava or semolina. And it is had in various forms, day in and out in the arid areas. Sometimes a batti is stuffed with vegetables or added to a pulao. This unusual dish is very much appreciated by non-Rajasthanis who go to specialised restaurants to eat it.

FOR THE GATTA

300	gms. gram flour
1	tsp. black pepper coarsely ground
1	tsp. cumin seeds coarsely ground
A pinch of ajwain	
2	tbsps. pure ghee

FOR THE PULAO

600	gms. basmati rice
100	gms. carrots cut julienne
100	gms. green peas boiled
15	baby potatoes boiled and fried whole
100	gms. seedless raisins
2	onions
6	red chillies ground in water

- Mix the gram flour, after sieving, with salt, pepper, cumin and ½ cup of pure ghee. Sprinkle some water, apply ghee to your hands and knead well until you obtain a stiff dough. Taste for salt.

- Make small, equal sized pieces of the dough and roll each on a clean wooden board to obtain a cylinder form like one's little finger.

- Boil three litres of water, add salt and drop in the dough strips and cook for atleast 10 minutes till the gatta is well cooked. Strain into a colander and chop each into smaller pieces. Do not allow them to stick.

2	tsps. garam masala
1	cup fresh coriander leaves chopped
½	cup fresh mint leaves
6	green cardamoms crushed
5	bay leaves
4	cloves lightly crushed
4	mace flowers

Salt

Pure ghee

- Cook the rice in the rice cooker along with the bay leaves, green peas, carrots and 1 tablespoon of ghee.

- Heat 1 cup of pure ghee in a vessel. Heat over medium flame and fry the whole potatoes in it. Remove from the vessel and put the chopped onion in it. When soft and brown add the whole spices — cardamoms, cloves and mace flowers. Cook for 3 minutes and pour in ½ a cup of ghee. When hot, gently drop in the cooked gattas and lightly fry from side to side. Sprinkle in the garam masala and add the chilli paste and fry. Add 2 tablespoons of water and lower the flame. Stir well and add the cooked rice with the green peas and carrots. Stir gently. Cook for 5 minutes over very low heat.

- Serve the gatta pulao hot in a salver. Surround it with the fried baby potatoes and sprinkle over the fried raisins. Stud with mint leaves.

Accompaniments:

A herbed raita

Cabbage and onion salad

A thin dal

Jalebis.

RAJASTHANI VEGETABLE PULAO

FOR THE RICE

500	gms. basmati rice
6	bay leaves
Salt	
Pure ghee	

FOR THE VEGETABLE GRAVY

100	gms. frenchbeans stringed and cut into ½" pieces
100	gms. carrots peeled and chopped into ½" pieces
100	gms. potatoes peeled and cut into small cubes
50	gms. cauliflower cut into small florets
50	gms. boiled green peas
2	onions finely chopped
2	onions sliced
2	tsps. sugar
6	green cardamoms crushed
6	cloves
1"	piece cinnamon broken into two
10	black peppercorns
1	tsp. carraway seeds
1	tsp. anise seeds
1	tsp. chilli powder
1	tsp. turmeric powder
1½	tbsps. garam masala
Salt	
Oil	
Pure ghee	

FOR THE GROUND MASALA

7	long green chillies deseeded
15	cloves garlic crushed
2"	piece ginger crushed
1	tbsp. broiled cumin seeds
1	tbsp. broiled coriander seeds
1	tbsp. broiled anise seeds

Grind in half a cup of water

FOR THE DECORATION

1	cup finely chopped fresh coriander
½	cup fresh mint leaves

- Wash the rice and set aside.
- Deep fry 2 sliced onions in a frying pan till golden brown and crisp. Fry potatoes in the same oil.
- Take 3 tablespoons of pure ghee and put it in a large vessel over a medium flame. When hot, toss in all the whole spices such as cardamoms, cloves, cinnamon, peppercorns and carraway seeds. Lower the flame, stir for 2 minutes and add the chopped onions and cook till soft and pink.
- Grind the masala to a buttery softness and add to the chopped onions and cook over a low flame for 5 minutes. Add all the vegetables, one by one into the pan and mix well. Add salt. Cook for 5 minutes and then sprinkle in the chilli and turmeric powders and the garam masala. Add a 1 cup of water or so, cover with a lid and pour some water on the lid and cook over a very low flame. Keep checking the vegetables so they don't dry up and keep pouring a little water at a time into the vessel from the lid. Cook till soft and tender. Sprinkle the sugar on the vegetables and stir gently.
- Cook the rice in the rice cooker along with the bay leaves, salt and half a cup of pure ghee. When fluffy and tender, add to the cooked vegetables, cover with a lid and heat over a very low flame for 10 minutes.
- Open the vessel at serving time and mix the rice and vegetables gently. Serve decorated with the chopped coriander and mint leaves.

Accompaniments:

Banana Raita

Potato Salan

Beetroot and Onion Salad

Mung Dal Halwa

AFLATOON LAL PULAO

FOR THE RICE

800	gms. basmati rice
4	bay leaves
1	cup coriander finely chopped
2	cups onions sliced deep fried
6	curry leaves finely chopped
1	cup seedless raisins fried

Salt
Ghee

FOR THE POTATOES

20	baby potatoes boiled in their skins in salted water
15	baby onions skinned deep fried
1	cup tomato ketchup
3	cups fresh tomato pulp
½	cup grated jaggery
2	golden peppers cut julienne

Salt
Ghee

FOR THE GROUND MASALA

10	red kashmiri chillies deseeded	
1	very large pod garlic	Ground in half a cup of vinegar
2	tbsps. cumin seeds	
2	onions chopped	
4	green chillies deseeded	
15	black peppercorns	
1	tsp. mustard seeds	

• Grind the masala to a very fine paste and set aside. Reserve the water with which you wash your mixie or grinding stone.

• Deep fry the baby onions and set them aside. Skin the boiled baby potatoes and deep fry them and set aside.

• Cook the rice along with the bay leaves, salt and 1 tablespoon ghee in a rice cooker.

• Place 2 tablespoons of ghee in a vessel and place over a medium flame. When the ghee gets hot, add the masala paste and lower the heat and fry the paste non-stop. Add the tomato ketchup and the fresh tomato pulp and mix non-stop for 5 minutes. Taste for salt. Add the jaggery, mix well for 3 minutes and gently add the fried baby onions and potatoes and allow to simmer for 7 minutes.

• Place the rice in a thali and quickly mix in the fried onions and raisins. Heat ½ tablespoon of ghee in a saucepan and add the curry leaves and allow to crackle for 2 minutes. Add the chopped coriander and put it and the curry leaves into the rice and mix well.

• Place the hot rice on a flat dish and top it with the potato-tomato mixture. Cover with the golden peppers, lightly fried, and serve hot at once.

Accompaniments:

Raw Mango and Onion Salad
Egg Curry
Buttered Mushrooms
Fried Ladyfingers
Raisin Ice-cream

BRINJAL SANDWICH PULAO

• Preparation Time: 20 mins. • Cooking Time: 55 mins. • Serves: 4-6

FOR THE RICE

500	gms. basmati rice
4	bay leaves
4	cloves
one pinch yellow colour	
Salt	
Ghee	

FOR THE BRINJALS

2	black, seedless brinjals atleast 6" to 8" long
3	sprigs curry leaves
2	sour limes
1	tbsp. turmeric
1	cup gram flour
1	pinch red chilli powder
Salt	
Oil	

FOR THE STUFFING MASALA

4	green chillies deseeded
1	cup chopped fresh coriander
1	tbsp. fresh mint
2	tbsps. grated coconut
1	tbsp. sesame seeds
1	tsp. cumin
1	tsp. sugar
Juice of 1 sour lime	

Grind very fine with the help of the lime juice

FOR THE GRAVY

700	gms. red tomatoes skinned pulped
2	medium onions
½	coconut grated
6	red kashmiri chillies deseeded
½	cup broken cashewnuts
1	tbsp. broiled coriander seeds
1	tsp. each grated ginger and garlic
2	tsps. sugar

Grind fine with little water

• Cook the rice with all its ingredients in a rice cooker.

• Grind the brinjal masala and gravy masala till fine.

• Chop the onions finely and place in a vessel with the curry sprigs and 2 tablespoons of ghee. Cook over a medium flame till soft and pink, then fry the gravy masala with the onions for 5 minutes. Lower the flame and mix the masala so it does not stick to the vessel. When red add the tomatoes, salt, lower the heat and allow to simmer for 10 minutes.

• Skin the brinjals and cut into ½" thick slices. Cut each slice into two with a sharp knife leaving the bottom attached. Apply salt, turmeric and sprinkle the lime juice over the brinjal slices. Place the green masala between each cut brinjal slice and stuff it as well as you can.

• Place half a karhai of oil to heat on a stove. Make a thin batter of the gram flour and water. Add salt and one pinch chilli powder. Mix well. The batter should be of a thin consistency.

• When the oil is hot, reduce the heat a little. Dip each brinjal slice separately in the batter and immerse it in the hot oil till the batter balloons out like a puri. Cook over medium heat as the brinjal needs to be cooked till soft. When golden in colour dip each sandwich in the warm tomato gravy. Finish all the brinjal slices in this manner.

• Divide the rice into two portions. Grease the bottom of a vessel and place half the rice in it. Sprinkle over it a pinch of yellow colour, the tomato gravy, brinjal sandwiches and cover with the remaining rice. Seal with a lid and dough and place on an iron tava for 20 minutes over a medium flame. Serve hot.

Accompaniments:

A thick Dal, Fried Tomato-Potato Salan

Hot Mango Pickle, Carrot Halwa

LILY CUP PULAO

FOR THE RICE

400	gms. basmati rice
2	green cardamoms
2	star anise
2	onions sliced and deep fried

One pinch saffron colour
Salt
Ghee

FOR THE LILY CUPS

9	large tomatoes cut into lily shape and the seeds and flesh scooped out

Salt
Butter

FOR THE STUFFING

300	gms. paneer cut into small cubes
100	gms. boiled green peas
2	tbsps. fresh mint leaves chopped
1	large pinch saffron strands broiled and added to a cup of hot milk
2	cups coconut milk
2	chopped onions

Salt
Ghee

FOR THE GROUND MASALA

150	gms. broken cashewnuts	Grind
1	tbsp. cumin	in a
1	tsp. grated ginger	little
6	green chillies deseeded	water

DECORATION

Almond slices — fried
Large raisins — fried

- Place the rice along with the cardamoms, star anise, the fried onions, salt and ghee in a rice cooker and cook till tender and fluffy. Divide into two parts and mix the saffron colour in one part. Stir lightly and place both the divisions back in the cooker to keep warm.

- Cut the large tomatoes into lily shaped cups. Remove the seeds and pulp and use it for another recipe. Sprinkle the tomatoes with salt.

- Place the 2 finely chopped onions in a vessel along with 1½ tablespoons ghee. Cook till soft and add the ground masala and fry for 5 minutes. Add 2 cups of coconut milk and allow to simmer for 5 minutes. Add salt, paneer and peas. Lower the fire and simmer till thick and dry.

- Take an aluminium tray or a pyrex rectangular, large dish or 2 smaller dishes. Grease with butter. Fill the tomato cups with the paneer and pea mixture and place in a pre-heated oven at 350°F for 25 minutes or until golden coloured.

- Reheat the rice in the rice cooker after sprinkling some water on it. Mix the white and saffron rice and place on a flat salver and place the baked tomato cups on it. Sprinkle with almond slices and raisins.

Accompaniments:

Thick Spicy Dal
Apple Salad with Spring Onions and Cucumber
Mango Barfi

PULAO DAHI-BADAM KA NAZAKAT

FOR THE RICE

2	gms. saffron
450	gms. basmati rice
2	onions sliced fried
1	tsp. coarsely ground cinnamon, cloves and cardamom seeds
1	tsp. allspice corns
Salt	
Ghee	

FOR THE PULAO

500	gms. tomatoes skinned chopped
200	gms. sliced mushrooms
200	gms. sliced cauliflower florets
200	gms. carrots sliced julienne
200	gms. frenchbeans sliced julienne
100	gms. green peas (boiled)
100	gms. sweet potatoes peeled and cubed
100	gms. white gourd peeled and cubed
100	gms. sweet brown raisins washed
100	gms. black seedless raisins washed
1½"	ginger cut julienne
1	bunch spring onions cut julienne
3	small red onions cut julienne
2	cups fresh coriander cut fine
½	cup fresh mint cut fine
2	tsps. sugar
Salt	

• Cook both the saffron and white rice separately. Cool on 2 large thalis.

• Take the spring and red onions and place them in a large vessel along with 4 tablespoons of ghee. Cook till the onions are soft and pink. Lower the heat and add the masala and stir-fry for 5 minutes. Then add the vegetables in the order that I write. First add the ginger and stir for 2 minutes. Then add the carrots, frenchbeans and white gourd and allow to cook over a low fire for 7 minutes. Add the reserved water from the mixie or grinding stone, stir well, add the cauliflower and sweet potatoes, add 2 cups of water and salt to taste and cook till tender. You must cover the vessel with a lid and pour water on it and keep watching that the bottom of the vessel is clear and not burnt or sticky. Keep adding the hot water from the lid as and when necessary. This should take atleast 30 to 45 minutes depending on your stove heat. The lower it is the better.

• When your vegetables are cooked, they should not be mushy but be al dente. Add the chopped tomatoes, the mushrooms, green peas and the 2 kinds of raisins and cook till about 1 to 2 cups of gravy is left. Remove from the fire.

• Take a large well-greased biryani vessel and place the white rice at the bottom of it. Spread all the cooked vegetables in a thick layer on top of the rice. Cover this with a layer of all the saffron

FOR THE MASALA

10	kashmiri chillies	
1	pod garlic	
¼	cup dried kopra grated	
2	tbsps. broiled coriander seeds	
2"	cinnamon	Grind in
1	tbsp. black peppercorns	1 cup
1	tbsp. poppy seeds	water
1	tbsp. fennel seeds	
1	cup toasted almonds	
½	cup toasted cashewnuts	
½	cup melon seeds	
½	cup cucumber seeds	

Retain the water in which the mixie or grinding stone is washed

FOR THE TOPPING

1 cup almonds boiled sliced fried
750 gms. yogurt whipped with 2 tsps. of sugar
750 gms. malai or clotted cream
½ cup pink rose petals

rice. Whisk the yogurt, malai and sugar and sprinkle it over the rice. Then sprinkle the rose petals and the sliced almonds. Tightly cover the vessel with a lid and dough. Place on an iron tava over a medium flame for 25 minutes. Serve carefully with the help of a porcelain quarter plate so that your guests all get the rice, vegetables, malai-yogurt and nuts in equal portions.

Accompaniments:

Paneer Tikkas

A cooked Vegetables Salad with Pears and Apples

Mango and Jaggery Chutney

Vanilla Ice-Cream and Orange Segments filled in orange shells

LARGE CHILLI STUFFED PULAO

• Preparation Time: 30 mins. • Cooking Time: 50 mins. • Serves: 6-8

FOR THE RICE

600	gms. basmati rice
150	gms. potatoes skinned cubed
100	gms. carrots skinned cubed
2	deep onions sliced fried
½	cup fried raisins
3	crushed green cardamoms
½	tsp. carraway seeds
Salt	
Ghee	

FOR THE CHILLIES AND THE GRAVY

15	large fleshy triangular shaped chillies 3"-4" long
2	onions chopped
1	cup medium to thin tamarind water
1	cup jaggery grated
1	tsp. red chilli powder
1	tsp. cumin broiled ground into powder
1	tsp. mustard seeds broiled ground
Salt	
Refined oil	

FOR THE CHILLI STUFFING

1	cup mashed potato	
½	cup crushed raw green peas	
½	cup crushed grated coconut	Grind till fine in ¼ cup water
6	green chillies deseeded	
½	cup raisins	
1	tsp. cumin crushed	
1	onion chopped	
2	sprigs curry leaves	
½	tsp. mustard seeds	
Refined oil		

• Cook the rice with all its ingredients in a rice cooker.

• Wash the chillies and slit them for an inch in the centre and remove the seeds. Wash and set aside.

• Grind the chilli stuffing coarsely and mix in the crushed raw green peas. Heat the onion and ½ tablespoon refined oil in a non-stick frying pan. When the onion starts getting soft add in the green peas mashed potato mixture and cook over very, slow heat for 12 minutes. Fill this stuffing into the chillies and lay them in a row at the bottom of a large vessel. Heat the curry leaves and mustard seeds in a karhai along with 1 tablespoon refined oil. When the mustard splutters pour the oil over the chillies and place the vessel over a very slow heat. Allow to sizzle for 5 minutes, add one cup of water, cover and cook till chillies are soft and tender.

• Place the 2 chopped onions with refined oil in a saucepan. Cook till the onions are pink. Lower the flame and add the chilli, cumin and mustard powders. Stir for 3 minutes and add the tamarind water and jaggery. Cook till the jaggery melts and the gravy becomes thick. Pour the gravy over the stuffed chillies. Cook for 5 minutes, allowing the chillies to simmer in the gravy.

• Place the rice in a salver and arrange the stuffed chillies over it. Serve very hot with any sweet murabba or chutney.

Accompaniments:

A Dal or Vegetable Curry

Salad of Apples, Bananas and Sweet Curd

Rabri with little Silver Mawa Balls

KARNATAKA'S BISI BELE HULI PULAO

• Preparation Time: 25-35 mins. • Cooking Time: 55 mins. • Serves: 8-10

FOR THE RICE
500	gms. basmati rice
250	gms. toovar dal
1"	cinnamon
4	green cardamoms lightly crushed
5	whole cloves
2	tbsps. ghee
Salt	

FOR THE VEGETABLE PULAO
50	gms. green peas
100	gms. carrots cubed
100	gms. frenchbeans cut into ½" pieces
100	gms. cauliflower florets
100	gms. brinjals cut into cubes
100	gms. sweet potatoes
100	gms. cabbage finely cut and fried
15	cloves garlic sliced
100	gms. tamarind pulp soaked in water
1½	tsps. turmeric powder
4	dried red chillies made into powder
4	onions sliced
3	sprigs curry leaves
1	tsp. (level) asafoetida (optional)
1	tsp. mustard seeds
Salt, Ghee	

FOR THE GROUND MASALA
3	tbsps. gram dal	
3	tbsps. urad dal	
2	tbsps. coriander seeds	Grind in a little water
4	red chillies/2 green chillies	
1½"	ginger	
1	tsp. fenugreek seeds	
½	cup dried kopra grated	

FOR DECORATION
½	cup freshly chopped coriander
2	tbsp. freshly chopped mint
100	gms. raisins
150	gms. whole small cashewnuts

• Wash the rice and toovar dal. Heat the ghee in a karhai and add the whole spices and fry, stirring all the time for 2 minutes. Add the rice and dal and fry for 5 more minutes and transfer them to a rice cooker. Add salt. Water should be carefully added so that the rice and dal are not mushy but cooked, fluffy and each grain is separate.

• Wash all the vegetables well. Take a very large vessel and add 1 cup ghee to it. Heat over medium flame. Add the mustard seeds, chillies, curry leaves and asafoetida and cook for 5 minutes in the vegetables except the cabbage and sweet potatoes, which should be fried separately in separate vessels. Fry the vegetable over a very slow fire and cook for ten minutes taking care to see that the bottom of the pan does not burn.

• Make two cups of tamarind water. Strain. Add to it the garlic and vegetables along with the turmeric and salt. Cover tightly with a lid. Place water on top of the lid. Keep checking on the vegetables and add hot water from the lid as necessary. When almost done add the ground masala mixed with half a cup of water and stir gently into the almost cooked vegetables. Put in the cabbage and fried sweet potatoes and dry up the gravy.

• Add the rice and dal to the cooked vegetables and mix gently and cover and keep for three to five minutes.

• Transfer to a flat dish, decorate with coriander, mint, raisins and fried cashewnuts.

Accompaniments:
Salad of beetroots and tomatoes

Sesame and lime chutney

Banana halwa

SADA METHI BHAJI AND PANEER PULAO

· Preparation Time: 15 mins. · Cooking Time: 40 mins. · Serves: 6-8

FOR THE RICE

500 gms. basmati rice
1½ tsps. cumin seeds broiled
Salt
Pure ghee

FOR THE METHI AND PANEER

3 bunches of large leafed methi or fenugreek leaves
500 gms. paneer best quality
2 medium onions finely chopped
Juice of 2 sour limes
1 tbsp. sugar
2 sprigs curry leaves
Salt
Pure ghee

FOR THE GROUND MASALA

1 medium onion
6 green chillies deseeded
15 large garlic cloves   } Grind fine in onion juice
10 black peppercorns
4 cloves
1" piece cinnamon

FOR DECORATION

200 gms. cream

- Cook the rice in a rice cooker with all its ingredients.

- Clean the methi bhaji and use mostly the leaves. Wash 2 to 3 times. Place water in a vessel to boil. Add salt to it and a pinch of soda bicarb. Add the fenugreek leaves and boil for 5 minutes on a high flame. Remove from the fire and drain in a colander till cool.

- Grind the fenugreek leaves, put it in a bowl, mix in the lime juice and sugar.

- Fry the curry leaves onions in 2 tablespoons ghee. When the onion becomes pink and soft add the ground masala and cook on low heat for 7 minutes, stirring all the time. Add the ground fenugreek leaves and allow to simmer for 5 minutes. Remove from the heat.

- Place the rice in a large thala.

- Chop the paneer into 1" cubes and fry in pure ghee till golden brown. Drain in a colander and mix into the rice.

- Take a large rectangular pyrex dish and grease it with white butter or ghee. Divide the rice into 2 portions. Place 1 layer of it in the dish. Then pour the cooked fenugreek in a neat layer. Lightly beat the cream and sprinkle half of it over the fenugreek bhaji. Cover with the remaining rice, level it and top the dish with the remaining cream. If you do not have a large pyrex dish arrange the pulao in 2 small dishes.

- Bake in an oven for 10 minutes at 350°F.

Accompaniments:

Onion and Radish Salad
Thick Masala Gravy with Guvarphalli
Black Masoor Salan
Shrikhand

PUNJABI PANEER PULAO

· Preparation Time: 20 mins. · Cooking Time: 1 hour · Serves: 6-10

FOR THE RICE

1	gm. saffron
500	gms. basmati rice
1	tsp. cumin seeds broiled
1	tsp. coriander seeds broiled
4	bay leaves
2	large brown cardamoms
3	star anise

Salt
Pure ghee

FOR THE PANEER GRAVY

500	gms. creamy rich paneer cut into 1" squares or 1½" rectangles
300	gms. medium sized onions sliced
300	gms. tomatoes skinned
1	cup fresh coriander leaves washed finely chopped
½	cup mint leaves

A pinch of ajma or ajwain
Salt
Pure ghee

FOR THE GROUND MASALA

3	green cardamoms seeds only	
10	black peppercorns	Grind in a little water
4	kashmiri chillies deseeded	
2	small onions	
1½"	ginger	
1	whole pod garlic	

FOR THE DECORATION

100 gms. whole cashewnuts

· Wash the rice and drain it. In a karhai heat 2 tablespoons of pure ghee and fry the cumin seeds, coriander seeds, bay leaves, star anise, brown cardamoms and the rice. Place in a rice cooker along with salt. Heat the saffron on a skillet and crumble it into the rice. Cook till tender.

· Heat half a frying pan of pure ghee and delicately fry the paneer and set aside and allow oil to drain. In the same ghee fry the sliced onions till golden and crisp. Place in a colander to drain along with the paneer.

· Roughly chop the tomatoes and place them in a large vessel. Add 3 tablespoons of the paneer-and-onion-fried ghee and cook on a medium flame. Add the ground masala and lower heat. Cook for 7 minutes and then add the chopped coriander and deep fried onions to the tomato mixture. Add salt to taste. When the tomatoes and masala are cooked, gently add in the paneer and stir. Cook on a very low heat for 5 minutes.

· Grease a straight sided biryani-type vessel on the bottom and sides. If you have a large pyrex bowl use that. Place a layer of rice at the bottom, then a layer of paneer, a layer of rice, a layer of paneer and top with the rice. Brail the ajwain and sprinkle on top of the rice along with the mint and fried cashewnuts.

· Heat in an oven for 10 minutes at 350°F and serve.

Accompaniment:

Curd "Kadhi" with Pakoras
Cucumber Raita and Mint Chutney
Mango Pickle with Saunf
Cold Apple Pudding

GOANESE MASALA STUFFED BRINJAL PULAO

• Preparation Time: 20 mins. • Cooking Time: 45 mins. • Serves: 4-6

FOR THE RICE
300 gms. basmati rice
Salt
Ghee

FOR THE BRINJALS
9   brinjals sweet and seedless with small thorns on the stalks
3   medium onions finely chopped
3   large tomatoes skinned and chopped
2   tsps. garam masala
3   sprigs curry leaves
1   tbsp. turmeric
Oil
Salt

FOR THE GROUND MASALA
3   tbsp. fresh coconut grated
6   green chillies deseeded
6   red dried chillies deseeded
12   large cloves garlic
1   small piece cinnamon
12   black peppercorns
4   cloves
4   green cardamoms seeds only
1   tbsp. tamarind
1   tbsp. jaggery

Grind in a ¼ cup of water

• Grind the masala till soft and buttery. Wash the rice and brinjals and set aside.

• The brinjals should be at least 3" long, thick and egg shaped. Cut the stem 1" above the brinjal. Remove all the thorns, then cut into 4 and stop 1" from the stem. Salt the brinjals lightly inside and out. Apply the turmeric powder same way.

• Stuff the ground masala, as much as you can and tie the brinjals with string.

• Make the brinjal gravy. Place the finely chopped onions in a vessel. Cook till soft in 2 tablespoons of oil and add the curry leaves, tomatoes and the garam masala. Once the gravy is pulpy add any remaining ground masala that you have from the brinjals. Lower the flame, add half a cup of water and cook the gravy till thick.

• Place the brinjals in 2 cups of hot water, salt and 1 tablespoon of oil and cook till soft. Add the tomato gravy a little at a time till the brinjals have become soft and only the gravy remains.

• Cook the rice till it is three-quarter cooked. Transfer to a rice cooker along with salt and 1 tablespoon of pure ghee. Add water accordingly. When ready, grease a large vessel with ghee and transfer the rice into it. Smooth the top of the rice and gently lay the stuffed brinjals over it. Pour all the remaining gravy over the brinjals. Seal the vessel with an airtight lid and dough. Place the vessel over very low heat for 35 minutes. Allow to settle for 10 minutes and serve hot.

Accompaniments:
Paneer Tikkas
Stuffed Ladyfingers
Whole Baby Mango Pickle
Rice Pancakes stuffed with Sweet Coconut

GUJARATI BRINJAL PULAO

• Preparation Time: 10 mins. • Cooking Time: 35 mins. • Serves: 6-8

FOR THE RICE

400	gms. basmati rice
3	bay leaves
4	green cardamoms lightly crushed
1"	piece cinnamon
Salt	
Ghee	

FOR THE BRINJALS

300	gms. brinjal skinned finely cut
2	large onions finely chopped
½	cup fresh coriander chopped
2	tbsp. mint chopped
2	sour limes for juice
1	tbsp. sugar
2	sprigs curry leaves
Salt	
Ghee or oil	

FOR THE GROUND MASALA

8	green chillies deseeded	⎫ Grind
6	black peppercorns	⎬ in
3	tsps. coconut freshly grated	} ¼ cup of water
2	tsps. roasted cashewnuts	⎭

• Wash the rice and cook with the bay leaves, cardamoms, cinnamon, salt and ghee till three-quarter cooked in the rice cooker. Add water accordingly.

• Chop the onions till fine. Place in a heavy-bottomed vessel with 2 tablespoons of oil and cook on medium heat till the onions are soft and pink. Add the curry leaves, fry for 2 minutes and then add salt and the brinjals. Lower the heat, cover and cook for 7 minutes. Add the ground masala and mix well and cover and cook for 10 minutes. If necessary, add a cup of water till the brinjal is as soft as pulp. Add the limejuice, coriander and mint.

• Add the rice after mixing it well on top of the brinjal. Sprinkle the top with a little water and pure ghee. Cover tightly with a lid on which water is added and place over a very low fire and cook till the rice has become tender. Serve hot with papads.

Accompaniments:

Cauliflower Vegetable cooked in coconut milk
Green Salad of White Radish with fresh dill
Curd with Spring Onions
Green Almond Wheat Milk Halwa

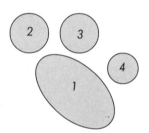

1. Pepper Splendour Pulao
2. Sautéed Cauliflower
3. Boondi-Potato-Pineapple Raita
4. Kaju Katli

JENNY'S EAST INDIAN VEGETABLE PULAO

• Preparation Time: 20 mins. • Cooking Time: 1½ hours • Serves: 6-8

My friend Jenny Patell gave me this recipe for vegetable pulao. Very simple, all the spices come from a bottle — the famous East Indian Bottle Masala which contains 22 to 25 items. They are kashmiri chillies, reshampatti chillies, madras chillies, black pepper, mustard seeds, cinnamon, cardamom, fennel seeds, lentils, saffron, mace, cumin, sesame seeds, cloves, turmeric, star anise, fenugreek seeds, allspice corns, bay leaves and ground wheat. With such a spectacular list no other masalas are needed.

FOR THE RICE

500	gms. long rice
2	bay leaves
Salt	

FOR THE VEGETABLES

50	gms. green peas
100	gms. french beans chopped
100	gms. carrots chopped
50	gms. cauliflower chopped
50	gms. capsicum chopped
2-3	green chillies deseeded
3	crushed cardamoms
2	large onions finely chopped
2½	tbsps. bottle masala
1	tbsp. pure ghee
1½	tbsps. refined oil
Salt	

• Take a large vessel with a heavy bottom and put in the oil and ghee. Place on a medium heat. Wash all the vegetables well, drain and put it in the hot oil along with the bottle masala and salt. Stir-fry the vegetables non-stop till almost soft. Add the crushed cardamoms and place on a very slow flame for 7 minutes.

• Chop the onions fine and cook in 1 tablespoon pure ghee over medium-low flame. Add the bay leaves and cook till soft and brown. Wash the rice and add it to the onions along with salt and fry for 7 minutes till well mixed with the onions. Then transfer the onions and rice mixture onto the cooked vegetables. Add sufficient water to cook the rice and cover tightly with a lid. Place water on the lid and cook over very low heat till the rice becomes fluffy and tender. Mix gently and serve.

Accompaniments:

Stuffed Potatoes

Capsicum Salan

Cucumber and Sweet Lime Raita

Coconut Cake with Jam Sauce

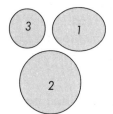

1. *Stuffed Masala Bhindis*
2. *Kurkuri bhindi (Crisp Ladyfinger) Pulao*
3. *Dal Bhajias*

SOONNA-NA-DANA-NO PULAO (GOLDEN BEAD PULAO)

• Preparation Time: 25 mins. • Cooking Time: 1 hour • Serves: 6-8

This is a lost and forgotten Parsi recipe. I doubt the last two generations have tasted it. I take this opportunity to place it before the reading public.

FOR THE RICE

2	gms. saffron
500	gms. basmati rice
6	cloves
10	black peppercorns
2"	cinnamon
3	crushed green cardamoms
2	bay leaves
2	star anise
1	tbsp. pure ghee
Salt	

FOR THE TOOVAR DAL

3	cups toovar dal
1	coconut — milk removed
1½	cups thick curd or yogurt
2	tsps. sugar
2	onions sliced and fried crisp
2	onions finely chopped
4	potatoes skinned and cubed ½" size
1	carrot skinned and cubed ½" size
3	tomatoes skinned and chopped
1	cup green peas boiled
6	green chillies deseeded and chopped
½	cup fresh coriander chopped
2	tbsps. fresh mint chopped
1½	tbsps. ginger garlic paste
2	tbsps. garam masala
1	tbsp. chilli powder
1	tbsp. turmeric powder
Salt, Ghee	

Accompaniments:

Mango Methi Pickle
Beetroot and Pearl Onion Salad
Sweet and Sour Brinjal Patia
Mango Shrikhand

• Cook the rice along with the saffron, cloves, peppercorns, cinnamon, cardamoms, bay leaves, star anise, salt and 1 tablespoon ghee in a rice cooker. When cooked spread it out on a thali.

• Wash the toovar dal. Allow it to boil in very hot water along with turmeric and salt, till soft — the dal grains should be intact. If they disintegrate, you will have to cook another batch of dal all over again. Drain the cooked dal in a colander.

• Take the 2 chopped onions and place them at the bottom of a vessel along with 1 cup of ghee. Place over medium flame and cook till soft and pink. Add the ginger garlic paste and mix well for 2 minutes. Then add the cubed potatoes and carrots and cook till soft by adding the coconut milk.

• When the potatoes have softened, add the garam masala, chilli powder, boiled green peas, chopped tomatoes, green chillies, fresh coriander and mint and stir gently for a further 7 minutes.

• Slowly fold in the drained toovar dal with the help of a saucer.

• Take a large vessel and apply ghee to the bottom and sides. Place half the cooked rice into it. Cover it with the toovar dal mixture and place the remaining rice over it. Cover with the two crisply fried onions.

• Whip the curd along with the sugar and pour it gently over the rice. Close the vessel with a lid and dough. Place over an iron tava for 20 minutes over medium flame till the rice comes to dum. Rest it for 10 minutes before opening it.

PARSI TARKARI NE MEWA (DRIED FRUIT) NO PULAO

• Preparation Time: 20 mins. • Cooking Time: 50 mins. • Serves: 8-10

FOR THE RICE

2	gms. saffron
600	gms. basmati rice
3	onions sliced and deep fried
4	mace flowers
1	tsp. carraway seeds
1	small piece cinnamon
Salt	
Ghee	

FOR THE VEGETABLES AND MEWA

200	gms. dried apricots	Place in
150	gms. golden raisins	sugar water
100	gms. dried figs	overnight
100	gms. black seedless currants	
200	gms. whole, fried cashewnuts salted	
100	gms. pine nuts fried	
50	gms. pumpkin seeds fried	
200	gms. potatoes skinned cubed and fried	
100	gms. green peas boiled	
100	gms. frenchbeans boiled cut	
100	gms. carrots boiled cubed	
2	large onions chopped	
3	large tomatoes skinned and chopped	
2	tbsps. fresh mint chopped	
½	cup curd or yogurt	
2	tsps. sugar	
Salt		
Ghee		

• Divide the rice into 2 portions. Cook 1 portion with saffron, half the onions, carraway seeds and mace flowers and the other half with the remaining fried onions, carraway seeds, mace flowers and salt in a rice cooker. Place both the rice in a large thala.

• Place the onions in a large vessel along with 3 tablespoons of ghee and cook over a medium flame till pink and soft. Add the fried potatoes, boiled vegetables and mint and allow to cook for 5 minutes over a low flame.

• Whisk the curd and sugar together and add the finely cut skinned tomatoes in a glass bowl. Then gently toss into the vegetables. Take large spoonfuls of white and saffron rice, alternatively, and mix into the vegetables.

• Boil all the dried fruits in their sugar water and sprinkle them into the vegetables and rice. Cover the vessel with a tight lid and dough and place over an iron tava for 20 minutes.

• Remove onto a flat dish and cover lavishly with the fried nuts.

Accompaniments:

Apple and Tomato Chutney with Red Chillies
Lettuce and Onion Salad
Channa Dal
Rabri

CORIANDER AND PANEER PULAO

• Preparation Time: 10 mins. • Cooking Time: 45 mins. • Serves: 4-6

FOR THE RICE

350 gms. basmati rice
2 onions sliced and deep fried
½ tsp. carraway seeds
Salt
1 tbsp. ghee

FOR THE CORIANDER AND PANEER

1 bunch coriander leaves
200 gms. paneer cubed
½ cup coriander freshly cut
2 bunches spring onions with 6" of the greens cut separately
1 large onion chopped
1 tbsp. fried pine nuts
Salt
Ghee

FOR THE GROUND MASALA

5 long green chillies deseeded
½ cup mint leaves
10 black peppercorns
1 tsp. broiled coriander seeds
½ tsp. broiled cumin seeds
Juice of 2 sour limes

} Grind very fine

• Cook the rice along with the fried onions, carraway seeds, salt and ghee in a rice cooker.

• Put the chopped onion along with 1½" tablespoons of ghee in a vessel and place on medium fire. When pink, add the chopped whites of the spring onions and after 5 minutes add the green portions finely chopped. Stir well until soft and then add the ground masala and briskly mix it up and down. Add the sour lime juice and the bunch of finely cut coriander. Lower the flame, add the cubed paneer after applying salt lightly, and cover the vessel. Pour water on the lid and cook for 5 more minutes.

• Toss the cooked rice into the vessel with the coriander mixture and allow the rice to absorb its essence.

• Lay the rice on a platter and top the rice with half cup of fresh coriander and the fried pine nuts.

Accompaniments:

Lemon Pickle in Oil

Capsicum Salad

Shahi Tukra

A SOUTHERN STYLE OMELETTE BIRYANI

• Preparation Time: 10 mins. • Cooking Time: 45 mins. • Serves: 4-6

FOR THE RICE

400	gms. basmati rice
2	onions sliced and deep fried
2	star anise
½	tbsp. ghee
Salt	

FOR THE OMELETTE

6	eggs – whisked
3	tbsps. onions grated
2	tbsps. raw mangoes grated
3	green chillies deseeded and finely chopped
3	tbsps. coriander finely chopped
1	tbsp. mint finely chopped
½	tsp. ginger garlic paste
½	tsp. turmeric powder
Salt	
Refined oil	

FOR THE MASALA

2	onions finely chopped
3	tomatoes skinned and finely chopped
100	gms. paneer cubed (½")
50	gms. raisins
½	tbsp. garam masala
1	tsp. chilli powder
½	tsp. turmeric powder
½	tsp. mustard seeds
½	tsp. cumin seeds
2	sprigs curry leaves
Refined oil	

• Cook the rice with the fried onions, star anise, salt and ghee in the rice cooker.

• Whisk the eggs in a glass or stainless steel bowl. Add all the chopped and grated items, ginger garlic paste, turmeric and salt. Heat oil in a non-stick frying pan and fry 3 omelettes out of the egg mixture. The omelette should be thick. Cut each into 1½" squares and set aside.

• Place the finely chopped onions in a large sauce pan. Add 2 tablespoons of oil and allow to cook over medium heat. When pink and soft, add the cumin and mustard seeds and curry leaves. Allow the seeds to splutter and add the garam masala, chilli powder, turmeric powder, tomatoes and raisins. Mix well and fry for 5 minutes. Add half a cup of water and make a thick gravy. Taste for salt and mix in the cubed paneer and set aside.

• Arrange half the rice in a vessel. Place the omelette pieces on top of it. Cover with the masala gravy and then the other portion of the rice. Cover with a well fitting lid and dough and place over an iron tava at medium heat for 20 minutes.

Accompaniments:

Sweet mango chutney

Beetroot, tomato and capsicum kachumber

Mango shrikhand

SPICED CAULIFLOWER AND SAFFRON PULAO

• Preparation Time: 15 mins. • Cooking Time: 50 mins. • Serves: 4-6

FOR THE RICE

2	gms. saffron
400	gms. basmati rice
200	gms. green peas
2	onions sliced and fried
4	bay leaves
4	large brown cardamoms
Salt	
Ghee	

FOR THE CAULIFLOWERS

8	baby cauliflowers. Keep 2-3 tender leaves attached to each one
1	coconut grated for milk
2	onions chopped fine
3	allspice leaves or bay leaves
Salt	
Refined oil or ghee	

MASALA FOR THE CAULIFLOWERS

10	kashmiri chillies	
15	large cloves garlic	
1	tbsp. cumin broiled	Grind
2	cloves	with
1"	cinnamon	half a
3	green cardamoms seeds only	cup of water
2"	ambahalad	
½	cup coriander freshly cut	

• Divide the rice into 2 portions. Cook one with half the fried onions, green peas, 2 bay leaves, 2 large brown cardamoms, salt and ghee. Cook the remaining portion with saffron, the remaining fried onions, 2 bay leaves, 2 large cardamoms, salt and ghee.

• Clean and wash the baby cauliflowers and soak in salted water for 10 minutes.

• Place the finely chopped onions in a vessel along with 2 tablespoons of ghee on a medium flame. Add the allspice or bay leaves and cook the onions till pink and soft. Add the masala to the vessel and briskly fry it up and down till it is well cooked. This will take 7 to 10 minutes. Add the coconut milk and lower the fire, add salt and the cauliflowers, half cover the vessel with a lid and cook till the cauliflowers are tender and the gravy is thick.

• Place the rice with the green peas on a silver salver and place the cauliflowers over it. Cover with the gravy and then the saffron rice.

Accompaniments:

Fried Fish or Mince

Yellow Tadka Dal

Cucumber and Coriander Raita

Custard Apple Basundi

SAVOURY PULAO

FOR THE RICE

2	gms. saffron
500	gms. basmati rice
3	onions sliced and fried
200	gms. green peas
100	gms. carrots cut into small cubes
100	gms. cauliflower small florets
100	gms. potatoes peeled and cubed
10	curry leaves
2	sour limes squeezed for juice
10	peppercorns
4	cloves
1"	cinnamon
3	green cardamoms seeds only

pounded finely

1½ tbsps. ghee
Milk of one whole coconut
Salt

FOR THE CHILLIES

12 large Saurashtrian type of chillies, which are fried and eaten with bhajias
1 tsp. cumin
Salt
Butter

FOR THE CHILLI STUFFING

100 gms. toovar dal
100 gms. potatoes
3 spring onions cleaned washed and cut julienne from the bulb to 5" above it
3 green chillies deseeded and cut fine
2 sour limes squeezed for juice
2 tbsps. sugar
1 tbsp. sambhar masala
Black rock salt
Butter

FOR THE DECORATION

16 fried whole cashewnuts

- Cook the rice along with the fried onions, green peas, carrots, potatoes, cauliflower, curry leaves, juice of 2 sour limes, the milk of 1 whole coconut plus as much water as necessary, pounded peppercorns, cloves, cinnamon and cardamom, salt and ghee in an electric rice cooker.

- Wash and dry the large chillies with a soft cloth. Cut them down one side and remove the seeds.

- To make the stuffing boil the dal in a pressure cooker with salt till dry. Boil the potato and mash it. Combine dal, potatoes and knead till smooth with buttered hands. Mix in the spring onions, cut green chillies, sour lime juice, sugar, sambhar masala and crushed black rock salt. Mix thoroughly and stuff the chillies.

- Heat 150 gms. of white or yellow butter in a karhai and when hot add the chillies gently to the butter and shake the vessel from side to side. Do not allow the chillies to brown.

- Lay out the hot vegetable rice in a glass dish and decorate it with the stuffed chillies and the fried cashewnuts.

Accompaniments:

Thick Parsi Dhansakh Dal

Eggs on Potatoes

Fresh Coriander Brinjal Salan

Vermicelli cooked in Milk and Nuts

GUCCHI — ALOO — AUR SAAG PULAO

FOR THE RICE

400 gms. basmati rice
1 tbsp. ghee
Salt

FOR THE VEGETABLES

200 gms. potatoes peeled and cut into ½" cubes and put in salted water
200 gms. mushrooms each cut into 4 pieces
1 bunch spinach, stalks removed
2 sprigs curry leaves
2 sour limes squeezed for juice
200 gms. onions finely chopped
1 cup coriander finely chopped
Salt
Refined oil

MASALA FOR THE VEGETABLES

1½ tbsps. ground cumin
6 green chillies deseeded and chopped
1 tbsp. sesame seeds broiled crushed
1 tbsp. coriander seeds broiled crushed
1 tsp. turmeric
1 tsp. chilli powder
2 tsps. garam masala

Mix together in a bowl

FOR THE DECORATION

Whole fried blanched almonds

• Cook the rice in an electric rice cooker along with the salt and ghee.

• Place the spinach in a vessel of boiling water to which you have added a pinch of soda-bicarb and salt. Drain in a colander.

• Place the onions along with the curry leaves and 2 tablespoons oil in a vessel. Cook over a medium flame till soft. Add all the dried masalas, lower the flame, and add the potatoes. Cook over a low flame. Cover the vessel and add a little water at a time to the potatoes and cook them till soft and dry. Add the mushrooms, the limejuice and the coriander, stir for 5 minutes and remove from the flame. Then toss in the hot spinach leaves and mix well.

• Place half the rice in a salver, cover with the vegetable mixture and the remaining rice. Top with whole fried, blanched almonds.

Accompaniments:

Black-eyed Peas with Vegetables
Salad of Fresh Pineapple and Green Lettuce
Baby Gulabjamuns in thin Semolina Sauce

MIXED VEGETABLE MINCE PULAO

• Preparation Time: 15 mins. • Cooking Time: 45 mins. • Serves: 4-6

FOR THE RICE

4	gms. saffron
400	gms. basmati rice
2	onions sliced and fried
3	cloves
3	green cardamoms lightly crushed
5	black peppercorns lightly crushed
1	tbsp. ghee
Salt	

FOR THE VEGETABLE MINCE

2	onions very finely minced or grated
100	gms. potatoes peeled minced or grated
100	gms. carrots peeled minced or grated
100	gms. cauliflower florets minced or grated
100	gms. tender cabbage minced or grated
10	cloves garlic minced or grated
2"	ambahalad or ginger minced or grated
1	teacup coriander chopped
¼	teacup mint chopped
3	sour limes squeezed for juice
3	tbsps. powdered sugar
2	tbsps. chat masala for sprinkling
2	tbsps. extra sugar
1	tbsp. garam masala for sprinkling
Salt	
Refined oil	

FOR THE STUFFED SWEET GREEN CHILLIES

15	green sweet chillies whole
2	curry sprigs
½	tsp. mustard seeds
Salt	
Refined oil	

• Mix all the chilli stuffing in a clean glass or stainless steel bowl. If necessary add 1 to 2 tablespoons or more of water. Add salt and mix vigorously.

• Slit the chillies along one side from top to almost the bottom. Keep the chilli twig intact at the top and the chilli intact at the bottom. Deseed, wash and dry with a soft cloth. Sprinkle fine salt and stuff the chillies with the thick gram flour mixture.

• Now cook the rice along with the saffron, fried onions, cloves, cardamoms, peppercorns, salt and ghee in a rice cooker.

• Take a large vessel. Add the onions and 2 tablespoons of refined oil and cook till soft. Add the extra sugar and cook till the onions are brown. Then add all the grated or minced vegetables including the ginger and garlic and salt. Lower the heat and cook over a very low fire. Cover with a lid and add water on it and cook the vegetables till tender. Every 10 minutes add the hot water from the lid and cook till the vegetable mince is soft. This will take 20 to 30 minutes over a low fire. Remove the vessel from the stove and mix in the coriander, mint, limejuice and sugar thoroughly. Then sprinkle the chat masala and garam masala into the vegetable mince, mix and keep covered.

• Take a large vessel and add 1 tablespoon oil to it. Heat it and add the curry sprigs and mustard seeds and allow them to splutter. Quickly add the stuffed chillies and shake the pan from left to right. Remove from the karhai. The chilli skins should not be charred but be glistening with oil.

STUFFING FOR THE SWEET GREEN CHILLIES

½ cup gram flour
½ cup water
2 sour limes squeezed for juice
4 small green chillies deseeded
1 tsp. cumin seeds broiled and coarsely ground
½ tsp. coriander seeds broiled and coarsely ground
½ tsp. fennel seeds broiled and coarsely ground
Salt
Refined oil

} Mix in a bowl

- Remove ²/₃ of the hot, cooked rice on a salver. Cover with the cooked minced vegetable and then cover with the remaining rice. Decorate with the stuffed chillies.

Accompaniments:

Melon salad
Potato raita
Gram dal paratha
Sweet saffron rava

RED PULAO WITH POACHED EGGS

FOR THE RICE

600	gms. long grained rice
2	cups tomato ketchup
4	green cardamoms crushed
4	cloves
3	star anise
3	bay leaves
1	tbsp. ghee
Salt	

FOR THE GRAVY

10	eggs
2	onions finely chopped
6	tomatoes skinned and pulped
2	sprig curry leaves
½	bunch coriander finely chopped
½	packet chives
Salt	
Sunflower oil	

FOR THE GRAVY MASALA

8	kashmiri chillies	
2	green chillies	
½	tbsp. coriander seeds broiled	Grind together with ½ a cup of water
½	tbsp. cumin seeds broiled	
½	tbsp. aniseeds broiled	
½	tsp. turmeric powder	
1"	fresh ambahalad	
10	large garlic cloves	
1	tbsp. sugar	

• Cook the rice along with the tomato ketchup, cardamoms, cloves, star anise, bay leaves, salt and ghee in an electric rice cooker.

• Chop the onions and put them along with the curry sprigs in a vessel with 2 tablespoons of oil. Cook them till soft and pink and add the finely ground masala and stir well over a low heat till the masala has cooked and emits a pleasant aroma. Add the pulped tomatoes, coriander and sugar and cook for 7 minutes till the sauce is ready. Taste for salt.

• Spread the cooked rice in a large vessel after greasing the base with ghee. Even the surface with a spatula and then spread the tomato sauce over the rice. Place over a low fire and make 10 dents in the rice. Crack an egg in each of the hollows. Sprinkle with the cut chives and fine salt and cover the vessel. Cook over a low flame till the eggs have set but not hardened. Serve immediately.

Accompaniments:

Potato and ladyfinger vegetable

Tomato and spring onion salad

Plain yogurt

Payasam for dessert

BUTTERED BABY VEGETABLE PULAO

• Preparation Time: 20 mins. • Cooking Time: 40 mins. • Serves: 6-8

FOR THE RICE

500	gms. long grained rice
2	onions sliced and deep fried
3	star anise
3	big black cardamoms
2	tbsps. sugar
1	tbsps. ghee
Salt	

FOR THE VEGETABLES

100	gms. baby Madras onions
100	gms. baby potatoes
100	gms. baby cherry tomatoes
100	gms. baby carrots
100	gms. baby gherkins (tendlis)
100	gms. cauliflower florets
3	onions finely chopped
5	tomatoes skinned deseeded and pulped
1	cup coriander finely cut
1	cup spring onions cut julienne
1½	cups thick cream
Salt	
Sunflower oil	

MASALA FOR THE VEGETABLE GRAVY

8	kashmiri chillies deseeded	
¼	fresh coconut grated	
1	cup broken cashewnuts	
10	black peppercorns	Grind in ½ a cup of water
1"	cinnamon stick	
4	cloves	
4	mace flowers	
½	tsp. carraway seeds	
1	tbsp. coriander seeds broiled	

FOR THE DECORATION

1	cup large raisins soaked in sugar water

• Cook the rice along with the fried onions, star anise, large cardamoms, salt and ghee in an electric rice cooker. Before switching it on place 2 tablespoons of sugar in a small vessel and allow to heat over a medium flame till the sugar burns to a golden brown colour. Pour in half a cup of water and mix well and add it to the items in the rice cooker. Mix and cook till the rice is brown and tender.

• Wash all the vegetables separately. Keep the baby tomatoes aside. Sprinkle with rock salt and fry each lot separately in a karhai of hot oil. Place in a colander so the oil drains out.

• Chop the onions finely and place in a vessel along with 1½ tablespoons of oil in which the vegetables had been fried. Cook till pink and soft and add the ground masala. Lower the flame and cook for 7 minutes mixing non-stop so that the masala does not stick to the bottom of the vessel. Add the tomatoes and the spring onions and cook till the tomatoes are soft and pulpy. One by one add the fried vegetables and stir gently into the masala. Taste for salt. Cook for 5 minutes over a low heat. Mix the baby tomatoes once the vegetables are covered in masala. Cover and set aside.

• Take a large vessel, which has a well fitting lid. Spread the brown rice on the base of the vessel. Spread it with a spatula and then cover it with the cooked vegetables. Whisk the cream lightly and sprinkle it on top of the vegetables. Cover with the lid and then seal it with dough. Place on a hot tava over a medium flame for 15 minutes. Rest for 7 minutes and then serve.

Accompaniments:

Grated White Radish Salad

Tomato Raita

Vegetable Cutlets

Malpooras with Raisins and Cream

HERBED EGG PULAO

· Preparation Time: 10 mins. · Cooking Time: 45 mins. · Serves: 6-8

FOR THE RICE

600	gms. long grained rice
½	tsp. shahjeera
4	mace flowers
1	tbsp. ghee
Salt	

FOR THE EGGS

8   boiled eggs halved
Large pinch pepper powder
Fine salt
Refined oil for frying

FOR THE EGG BATTER

½	cup gram flour
½	tsp. minced ginger
1	tsp. minced chives
1	tsp. minced parsley
1	tsp. minced spring onion whites only
1	tbsp. sour lime juice
1	tbsp. powdered sugar
Salt to taste	

· Cook the rice with all its ingredients in an electric rice cooker.

· Make a very thin batter with the gram flour and water. Add salt. Then mix in the ginger, chives, parsley, spring onions, lime juice and sugar.

· Place a vessel half filled with oil on a medium flame till hot. The batter should hold — do not over-thin-it. Dip each half egg piece in the batter and lower it into the hot oil. Fry all the egg pieces in batches of four till golden brown and place in a tray.

· Arrange the eggs on the hot rice in a dish.

Accompaniments:

Thick tomato curry

Sambar dal

Beetroot and onion salad

Cold rice payasam

TAMARIND AND DRUMSTICK PULAO WITH EGGS

• Preparation Time: 15 mins. • Cooking Time: 40 mins. • Serves: 6-8

FOR THE RICE

600	gms. basmati rice
2	onions sliced and fried
200	gms. fresh green peas
½	tsp. carraway seeds
1½	tbsp ghee
Salt	

FOR THE EGGS

12   whole boiled eggs
One pinch saffron colour
Fine salt
Refined oil

FOR THE TAMARIND AND DRUMSTICK GRAVY

1	cup tamarind pulp
1½	cups grated jaggery
4	drumsticks
2	onions finely chopped
1	tsp. turmeric
1	cup coriander freshly cut
2	tbsps. mint freshly cut
3	sprig curry leaves
½	tsps. mustard seeds
1	pinch asafoetida
Salt	
Refined oil	

MASALA FOR THE GRAVY

1	cup grated coconut	
10	kashmiri chillies deseeded	Grind
12	large garlic cloves	in
1½	tbsps. cumin seeds broiled	½ cup
1	tbsp. coriander seeds broiled	of water
1	tbsp. fennel seeds broiled	

• Cook the rice with all its ingredients in an electric cooker.

• Boil the eggs and allow to cool. Shell and set aside. Skin the drumsticks thoroughly and cut into 2" pieces. Boil in salted water till tender. Drain and set aside.

• Place the chopped onions in a vessel with 2 tablespoons of oil on medium heat. Add the curry sprigs and allow to cook till soft.

• Meanwhile boil the tamarind pulp and the jaggery along with 1 cup of water. Strain through a fine sieve and set aside.

• When the onion softens, add the turmeric and mustard seeds and allow them to splutter and then add the ground masala. Lower the flame and stir non-stop for a few moments till the cooked masala emits a pleasant aroma and pour in the tamarind – jaggery water and allow to simmer for 15 minutes.

• Add the asafoetida, coriander and mint. Taste for salt, sweetness and sourness.

• Fry the boiled eggs in a tablespoon of ghee to which you have added a pinch of saffron colour. Add them and the drumstick pieces to the gravy and remove the vessel from the heat.

• Lay half the rice in a vessel, cover with the necessary quantity of gravy, boiled eggs and drumsticks. Cover with the remaining rice. Place a lid on the vessel and seal with dough. Place the vessel on a tava over a medium flame for 15 minutes.

Accompaniments:

Masala Potatoes and Green Peas
Endive Salad
Stuffed Masala Brinjals
Cold Rice Kheer

KURMU (JACKFRUIT) PULAO

• Preparation Time: 20 mins. • Cooking Time: 50-55 mins. • Serves: 6-8

FOR THE RICE

500	gms. long grained rice
2	onions deep fried
2	potatoes peeled and cubed about ½"
2	carrots peeled and cubed about ½"
1	baby cauliflower cleaned and cut into florets
1	cup fresh green peas
1	tsp. cumin seeds broiled
1	tsp. coriander seeds broiled
4	mace flowers
1	tbsp. garam masala
	Sufficient coconut milk to cook the rice and vegetables
2	tbsps. ghee

A pinch of yellow pulao colour
Salt

FOR THE JACKFRUIT

750	gms. only fruit pieces intact after removing the seeds
2	onions deep fried
1	tsp. mustard seeds
½	cup tamarind and jaggery pulp
3	sprigs curry leaves
½	cup fresh mint chopped
1	cup cashewnuts fried salted

Peanut oil or ghee, Salt

FOR THE GROUND JACKFRUIT MASALA

10	deseeded green chillies
½	coconut grated
12	black peppercorns
1"	cinnamon
2	cups fresh coriander finely cut
2"	ambahalad or fresh ginger
10	garlic cloves
2	tbsps. sesame seeds

Seeds of 4 green cardamoms

Grind in ½ cup water

• Cook the rice in an electric rice cooker. Add the deep fried onions, vegetables, broiled cumin and coriander seeds, the mace flowers, garam masala, yellow pulao colour, salt and ghee.

• Either you boil the jackfruit or deep fry it.

• Heat the mustard seeds in 1 tablespoon of ghee. When they crackle, add the curry sprigs, stir and add the deep fried onions. Lower the flame and add the ground masala along with salt and mix vigorously till a lovely aroma comes forth. Add the tamarind — jaggery pulp and stir for 5 minutes and then add the boiled or fried jackfruit. Lower the flame and simmer for 10 minutes.

• Grease a vessel on the base and sides. Place half the rice inside and top it with the jackfruit gravy. Cover gravy with the remaining rice. Top with the mint and cashewnuts. Cover the vessel with a fitting lid and dough. Place it on a tava over medium heat for 15 minutes.

Accompaniments:

Fruit and cucumber salad
Brinjal Vegetable
Cabbage cooked with Peanuts
Rose Milk Sherbet

PEPPER SPLENDOUR

• Preparation Time: 20 mins. • Cooking Time: 45 mins. • Serves: 6

FOR THE RICE

450 gms. basmati rice
4 bay leaves
1 tbsp. ghee
Salt

FOR THE RICE GRAVY

1	cup boiled green peas	
1	onion deep fried	
½	grated onion	Grind
8	green chillies	finely
10	garlic cloves	in ½
½"	piece ambahalad	cup
½"	piece fresh turmeric	water
1	tbsp. broiled fennel seeds	
5	cashewnuts	
Oil		

FOR THE PEPPERS

4 red peppers
5 golden peppers
Salt
Oil

FOR THE PEPPER STUFFING

400 gms. red pumpkin finely cubed
200 gms. red carrots finely cubed
200 gms. sweet potatoes finely cubed
200 gms. onions chopped
400 gms. tomatoes finely chopped
½ cup coriander finely chopped
Juice of 2 sour limes
½ cup sugar
1 tsp. turmeric powder
1 tsp. black pepper powder
2 tsps. mixed cardamom, clove and cinnamon powder
2 tsp. jeera powder
3 curry sprigs
Refined oil

• Wash the rice and cook with all its ingredients in the electric rice cooker.

• Prepare the rice gravy by grinding the masala till soft. Place the fried onion in a vessel with 1 tablespoon oil and cook the masala gently over a medium flame for 5 minutes. Add salt and 2 cups of water and cook for 10 minutes. Then gently put in the boiled green peas. Taste for salt.

• Chop all the vegetables separately and deep-fry in hot oil. Drain in a large colander. Cook the onions in a vessel till soft then add the curry leaves and chopped tomatoes and all the powdered masalas. Cook for 5 minutes over medium heat. Gently mix in the fried and salted vegetables and cook for another 5 minutes. Dry. Remove from the stove and mix in the chopped coriander, lime and sugar mixture. Taste for salt.

• Wash and wipe the peppers and cut them carefully from around the stem in a circular incision and remove all the seeds. Then stuff them with the vegetable mixture. Oil the peppers lightly and place them in a pyrex dish with half a cup of water and bake at 350°F till soft.

• To serve, remove the hot rice in dishes, cover over with the gravy, make indentations in the rice and place the peppers in them.

Accompaniments:

Sautéed Cauliflower

Onion

Cucumber

Boondi Raita

Kaju Katli

STUFFED COCONUT KARELA (BITTER GOURD) PULAO

• Preparation Time: 25 mins. • Cooking Time: 45 mins. • Serves: 4-6

FOR THE RICE

500	gms. basmati rice
4	allspice leaves
1½	tbsps. ghee
Salt	

FOR THE RICE GRAVY

2	onions finely chopped
700	gms. tomatoes skinned finely pulped
1½	tsps. chilli powder
3	tbsps. ground coconut paste
2	tbsps. cashew paste
1	tbsp. ambahalad paste
1	tbsp. sugar
Salt	
Oil	

FOR THE KARELAS

8	karelas fresh and green about 3" in length
2	tbsps. lime juice
Salt	
Oil	

FOR THE KARELA STUFFING

1	large coconut, freshly grated
1	large potato boiled and mashed
½	cup seedless raisins
½	cup peanuts toasted coarsely crushed
½	tsp. mustard seeds
½	tsp. cumin seeds
1	tbsp. sugar
2	tbsps. lime juice
3	sprigs curry leaves
Salt	
Ghee	

• Wash the karelas and lightly remove their scrubby surfaces. Cut them on one side and remove the seeds and spongy centres. Then soak them in cold water, in which you have added 3 tablespoons of salt and the lime juice.

• Cook the rice in an electric rice cooker after adding the allspice leaves, salt and ghee.

• Make the rice gravy by cooking the chopped onions in a vessel to which you have added 2 tablespoons of ghee. When the onions have become soft and pink add the chilli powder, mix well and add the coconut paste, cashew paste and ambahalad paste and cook for 5 minutes over a low fire. Add the tomatoes, sugar and salt and raise the heat and allow the sauce to boil and thicken. If you like add 2 deseeded green chillies whilst boiling the gravy for taste. Remove from the fire when slightly thickened.

• Make the karela stuffing by placing 1 tablespoon ghee in a karhai. Drop in the curry leaves, the mustard seeds and the cumin seeds. Stir for 2 minutes and drop in the raisins and the peanuts and then the grated coconut and cook for 7 to 10 minutes till the coconut mix is soft enough to eat. Mix in the mashed potato, salt, sugar and lime juice, and if you like, 4 green chillies, deseeded and finely chopped. Then remove the mixture from the fire. Cool slightly. Taste for salt.

• Drain the karelas from the water and squeeze between both your hands and stuff them with the coconut mixture. Tie the karelas with thin white thread so the mixture does not ooze out. Then take a vessel, heat 2 tablespoons of ghee in it and when hot place the karelas in it and turn

them back to front for 7 minutes. Then keep sprinkling a little water at a time and cover them with a lid which holds water. Keep adding the hot water on the lid to the karelas till they become soft and tender.

- Place the hot rice in a dish, pour over as much gravy as you reasonably think fit and align the stuffed karelas on top.

- Serve with a raita, pickle, dal and chum-chum sweets.

KURKURI BHINDI (CRISP LADYFINGER) PULAO

• Preparation Time: 7 mins. • Cooking Time: 35 mins. • Serves: 4

FOR THE RICE

350	gms. basmati rice
1	onion sliced, deep fried
1	star anisé
2	crushed green cardamoms
½	tsp. crushed saffron
1"	cinnamon
10	black peppercorns
2	cloves
½	tsp. fennel
1	tablespoon pure ghee
salt	

Coarsely dry grind

FOR THE LADYFINGERS

300	gms. tender ladyfingers
1	tsp. chilli powder
1	tsp. sambhar powder
1	tsp. mango powder
1	tsp. chaat powder
1½	tsp. powdered salt
Refined oil	

• Cook the rice with the fried onion, star anisé and green cardamoms. Spread the rice in a thali and sprinkle the coarsely ground masala powder on it and mix well with your hands.

• Wash the ladyfingures, dry them with a soft tea napkin and cut each diagonally as shown in the picture. Spread out on a tray or thali and sprinkle the masala powder on top of the slices and mix lightly.

• Heat a karhai half filled with refined oil. When hot fry small batches of the slices till lightly brown and crisp. By frying small quantities they will not stick to each other. Drain on absorbent paper.

• Arrange the ladyfingres on the rice as shown in the picture within a circle of sweet lime slices.

Accompaniments:

Drumstick Salan

Masala Dal

Lemon Pickle

Raw Vegetable Salad

Rabri with cut Mango pieces

Other Cook books from Vakils, Feffer & Simons Ltd.:

Jamva Chaloji — *Katy Dalal*

Delicious Encounters — *Katy Dalal*

The Pleasures of Vegetarian Cooking — *Tarla Dalal*

The Joys of Vegetarian Cooking — *Tarla Dalal*

The Delights of Vegetarian Cooking — *Tarla Dalal*

Rotis and Naans of India — *Purobi Babbar*

Say Cheese for Better Health — *Purobi Babbar*

The Flavours of China — *Purobi Babbar*

Eat and Stay Slim with Soups and Salads — *Purobi Babbar*

Food Heritage of India — *Vimla Patil*

Aahar – Food Treasures of India — *Vimla Patil, Anita Patil*

Exotic Curries of the Orient — *Vimla Patil, Monisha Bharadwaj*

Enjoyable Parsi Cooking — *Jeroo Mehta*

Cooking Delights of the Maharajas — *Digvijaya Singh*

Vegetarian Party Menus — *Hemantika Puri*

Relish Food – The Vegetarian Way — *Vina Khandwala*

Eggless Cakes — *Rosalind Aloysius*

Enduring Flavours — *Michael Swamy Fernandes*